BEHIND THE SCENES
AT THE
MUSEUM

BEHIND THE SCENES
AT THE
MUSEUM

YOUR ALL-ACCESS GUIDE TO
THE WORLD'S AMAZING MUSEUMS

 SMITHSONIAN

Project Editor Amanda Wyatt
Senior Art Editor Jacqui Swan
Editors Alexandra Di Falco, Ben Ffrancon Davies
US Editor Megan Douglass
Designer Anna Pond
Writers Ben Ffrancon Davies, S.I. Martin
Consultant Jenny Pistella, Cultural Heritage Learning Consultant
Picture Researchers Liz Moore, Jo Walton, Sarah Hopper
Illustrator Philip Harris
Managing Editor Lisa Gillespie
US Managing Editor Lori Hand
Managing Art Editor Owen Peyton Jones
Production Editor Gillian Reid
Senior Production Controller Meskerem Berhane
Jacket Designer Akiko Kato
Publisher Andrew Macintyre
Art Director Karen Self
Associate Publishing Director Liz Wheeler
Publishing Director Jonathan Metcalf

First American Edition, 2020
Published in the United States by DK Publishing
1450 Broadway, Suite 801, New York, NY 10018
Copyright © 2020 Dorling Kindersley Limited
DK, a Division of Penguin Random House LLC
20 21 22 23 10 9 8 7 6 5 4 3 2 1
001–314323–June/2020

A catalog record for this book
is available from the Library of Congress.
ISBN 978-1-4654-9325-5

DK books are available at special discounts when purchased
in bulk for sales promotions, premiums, fund-raising, or educational use. For details,
contact: DK Publishing Special Markets,
1450 Broadway, Suite 801, New York, NY 10018
SpecialSales@dk.com

Printed and bound in China

For the curious

www.dk.com

Smithsonian

Established in 1846, the Smithsonian is the world's largest museum and research
complex, dedicated to public education, national service, and scholarship in the
arts, sciences, and history. It includes 19 museums and galleries and the National
Zoological Park. The total number of artifacts, works of art, and specimens in the
Smithsonian's collection is estimated at 155.5 million.

CONTENTS

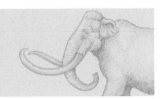

1

TREASURE TROVES

2

FINDING HISTORY

3

SORTING THE PAST

4

SAVING HISTORY

5

RESEARCH AND REPLICAS

6

SHOW AND TELL

TREASURE TROVES

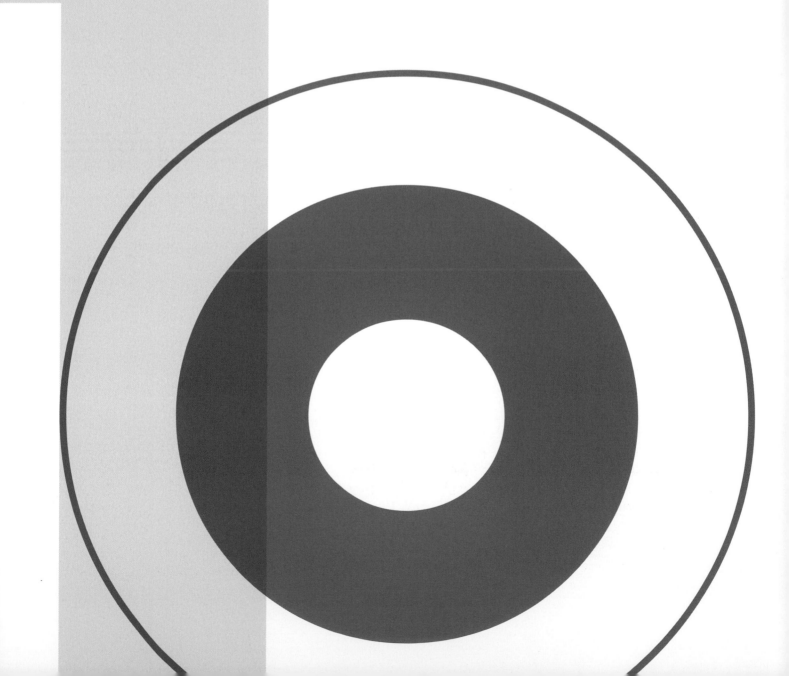

Museums are dedicated to preserving the past and present and collecting knowledge. They try and find exciting ways to explain that knowledge to everyone who walks through their doors. They come in all shapes and sizes, covering big subjects such as science and natural history, and obscure ones, too, such as miniature books and toilets. Running a museum takes a lot of work—up to hundreds of people with a huge variety of skills help to collect, restore, and care for artifacts and specimens. Artifacts are historical objects made by humans, while specimens are examples of animals, plants, or minerals collected for scientific research. Both types of items may then be put on display for the public to admire.

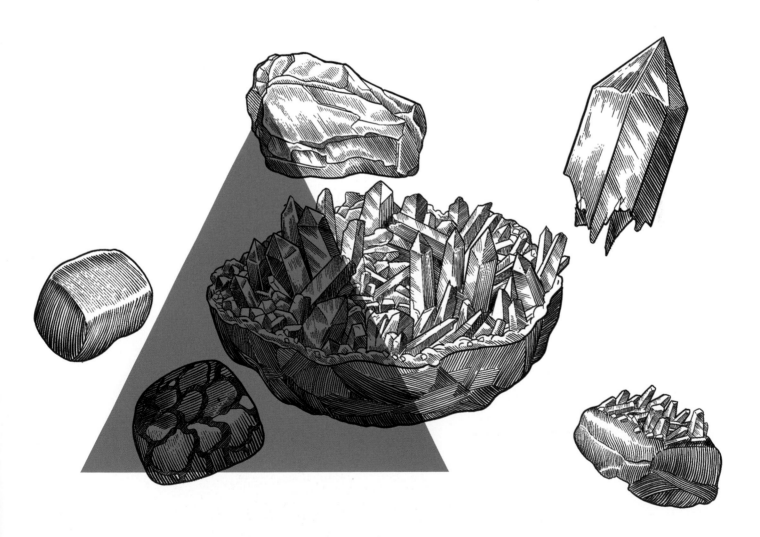

WHAT IS A MUSEUM?

Museums are much more than buildings full of dusty, old objects—they are places that tell us the stories of humans and our planet. They protect enormous collections of artifacts (objects made by humans) and specimens (natural things, such as animals, plants, or minerals). Museum researchers investigate these objects to find out more about them—then they share their knowledge with us.

▼ Engaging exhibit

This eye-catching animal exhibit, visible from all the floors of the Museum of the Sciences in Trento, Italy, brings natural history to life, wowing the public and showcasing the museum's fascinating collection.

Why do they do it?

Museums around the world employ thousands of people to look after their objects. It takes a lot of time and patience to care for the often fragile items in a museum's collection, but why do they do it?

Learning about the past

Museums show us some incredible items and, through them, teach us about our planet's unique past, from prehistoric rocks and skeletons to handmade objects that show us how our ancient ancestors once lived.

This 2,000-year-old jade burial suit from China remains in good condition thanks to museum preservation techniques.

JADE BURIAL SUIT

Preserving history

Museums look after objects that mark significant artistic, cultural, scientific, and technological developments in history. These objects act as a record of human endeavors over time and allow us and future generations to see how people have changed the world we live in.

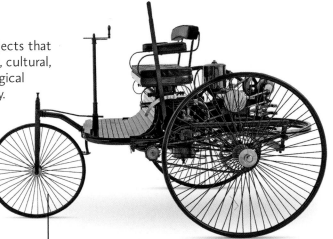

This three-wheeled vehicle is a replica of the original automobile.

BENZ PATENT-MOTORWAGEN

Donations

Some items in museums are much more personal. This collection of photographs and memorabilia was donated to the Warsaw Rising Museum, Poland, by the families of World War II survivors.

Research for the future

Many museums are centers of research. Scientists and historians study specimens, like these ancient insects preserved in amber, to learn more about the history of our planet, which can help us predict what might happen in its future.

This insect was caught in the tree sap and preserved when it hardened.

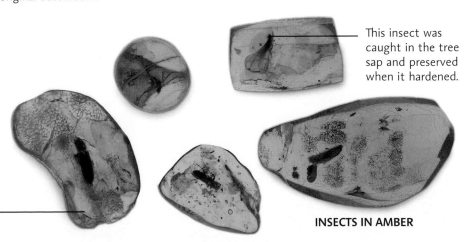

Amber is made of hardened tree sap.

INSECTS IN AMBER

ROOM OF WONDER

In 16th-century Europe, it became popular for the aristocracy—the powerful upper class—to create private collections known as "Rooms of Wonder" or "Cabinets of Curiosities." Other wealthy members of society often visited these "Rooms of Wonder" for entertainment. The collections were full of unusual human-made objects as well as animals, plants, and minerals. While some collections were for scientific or historical study—others were simply a selection of items that appealed to their owner's interests. Many of these personal collections later formed the basis of museums that opened in the 18th and 19th centuries.

Moving machine
This mechanical figure could bend forward and pick up objects placed before it.

Cabinet of curiosity

Ole Worm was a 17th century Danish physician and collector. His incredible cabinet of curiosities, known as the *Musei Wormiani*, included human-made objects, taxidermied animals, fossils, skeletons, gemstones, and dried plants, as well as many other items. He recorded the origin and estimated age of each item in his collection.

USEI
MIANI
STORIA
BATAVORUM
A ELSEVIRIANA
Typog: 1655.

METAL·LICA · · METALLA MINERALIA · P.

TURBINATA · CONCHILIA · MARIANA · LAPIDES

ANIMALIUM PARTES · CONCHILIATA · VARIA · SUCCI · FRUCTUS · SEMINA · LIGNA · COR

LAPIDES · LAPIDES

Arctic creature
The polar bear hanging from the ceiling beside a kayak reveals Worm's interest in the Arctic and the animals and people that lived there.

Early geology
Worm had a large collection of gemstones and minerals, which was later studied by geologists.

Seeds and dried plants
Worm wrote detailed notes about the seeds and dried plants he had in his collection.

WHAT IS A COLLECTION?

The objects that a museum cares for are known as its collection. A museum's collection can be made up of thousands, or even millions, of artifacts, so only a small fraction of them can ever be displayed to the public at one time. The rest are loaned out to other museums, used for research and study, or kept in storage. These objects from the Department of Anthropology collections at the Smithsonian National Museum of Natural History are kept in drawers at an off-site center in Maryland. They include examples of cultural objects such as clothes, toys, and decorative arts from around the world.

Densely packed displays

Some museums try to cram as much as possible into their displays instead of putting things in storage. The Ettore Guatelli Museum near Parma, Italy, makes a marvel out of the seemingly mundane, showcasing more than 60,000 everyday objects from farm tools (shown above) to clocks, and tin cans to glass bottles.

TYPES OF
MUSEUM

The world's museums cover almost every subject you could think of. Whatever you're interested in, you'll almost definitely be able to find a museum to satisfy your curiosity. To care for, research, and teach others about their collections, museums with a particular subject focus employ staff who have lots of knowledge about that topic. Here are just some of the different types of museum you can find around the world.

These butterfly specimens are stored at Berlin's Natural History Museum in Germany.

NATURAL HISTORY MUSEUMS

From dinosaurs to insects and fossils to meteorites, museums of natural history are homes to all kinds of animal, plant, and mineral specimens. They are also research institutions, dedicated to collecting, cataloging, and investigating the natural world. Though many of the specimens in their collections are very old, researchers can study them to find out more about our planet today, too.

MILITARY MUSEUMS

The history and experience of warfare is brought to life in military museums, with displays of weapons, armor, and uniforms. In military museums, visitors can explore the stories of the lives of soldiers and people who have lived through wars, from ancient conflicts to those of the present day.

This 16th-century armor is displayed at The German Historical Museum in Berlin.

SOCIAL HISTORY MUSEUMS

Cultural museums collect items that reveal details about how people and communities lived in the past and how they live now. These items might include clothing, tools, toys, or even entire houses. The Astra Museum near Sibiu in Romania has a collection of traditional rural houses, showing visitors the different types of dwelling found across the country.

WOODEN HOUSES AT THE ASTRA MUSEUM

HISTORY MUSEUMS

History museums showcase artifacts that reveal the stories of people and events in the past. They might cover the history of a huge geographical area, such as a continent, or a much smaller one, such as a village, or they might focus on a particular time period in history.

1930s POLISH FIGHTER PLANE AT THE POLISH AVIATION MUSEUM

This 16th-century sun stone sculpture is on show at the National Museum of Anthropology in Mexico.

TRANSPORTATION MUSEUMS

From planes and boats to cars and trains, transportation museums reveal how technology has developed over time to make transportation faster, cheaper, and more efficient. Transportation museums are often in disused airfields, depots, or train stations, like the Polish Aviation Museum in Krakow, shown here, which is housed in a former airport.

BEST OF THE REST

▶ MARITIME MUSEUMS

Maritime museums specialize in nautical history, with displays relating to voyages on water, shipping, piracy, and maps.

▶ DESIGN MUSEUMS

Eye-catching exhibitions on design, fashion, architecture, graphics, and product and digital design are showcased at design museums.

▶ VIRTUAL MUSEUMS

World-famous museums offer virtual visits to their extraordinary online collections of digitally recorded images, sound files, and text documents.

Made in 2000, this humanoid robot is known as ASIMO. It is on display at Japan's National Museum of Emerging Science and Innovation.

SCIENCE AND TECHNOLOGY MUSEUMS

In a science and technology museum, you'll find a breathtaking variety of objects—from ancient medical equipment to lunar modules. These museums keep a record of scientific discoveries and pioneering inventions.

MUSEUM DEPARTMENTS

It takes a lot of people with a huge range of specialized skills to make a museum work. From the adventurous archaeologists and the creative curators who work behind the scenes to the engaging visitor services and education staff that welcome curious visitors, museums couldn't open their doors every day without these talented teams of inquisitive individuals.

VISITOR SERVICES

Whether they are welcoming you to the museum, answering questions about exhibits, or giving a guided tour, a museum's visitor services staff are responsible for all the aspects of a museum that are on display to the public. They help visitors access and appreciate all there is to see in the museum. Without these friendly faces, museums could be difficult to navigate, and impossible to enjoy to their full potential.

COLLECTIONS MANAGEMENT

Teams in charge of collections management make sure that the precious and often fragile objects in museums are kept safe. This work can include advising on how to store or display an object, overseeing the packing and transportation of items that are going on loan to another museum, or carefully planning how certain objects should be cared for in the long-term.

CONSERVATION

All artifacts and specimens, particularly older ones, need careful conservation or they will deteriorate beyond repair. It's a conservator's job to care for, clean, treat, and preserve items to keep them in the best possible condition so that they can continue to be appreciated by future generations. These highly trained specialists learn how to care for items without damaging them.

CURATORIAL AND EXHIBITION

Of the sometimes millions of objects in a museum's collection, it is curators and exhibition teams that select exactly what should go on display to the public. It's thanks to them that objects are arranged in displays that are easy to understand and enjoyable to explore, supported by interesting information to help visitors discover more about what they're looking at.

OTHER TEAMS

There are many more departments that keep a museum going. Here are some others:

▶ **EDUCATION AND LEARNING**
As well as helping to host school visits, these teams arrange classes, courses, and workshops so visitors of all ages can learn about a museum's collection.

▶ **MARKETING AND COMMUNICATIONS**
When a museum puts on exhibits, these teams help spread the word and make sure as many people as possible know what's happening.

▶ **OPERATIONS**
Responsible for the day-to-day running of a museum, operations teams take care of finances, visitor safety, cleaning, and security.

▶ **PHOTOGRAPHIC SERVICES**
Some museums have photographers who take photographs for the organization's records and to track the condition of objects over time.

FINDING
HISTORY

Have you ever wondered how museums collect all of their incredible artifacts and specimens? Some are donated by individuals from their own private collections, but others have to be searched for long and hard. Archaeologists dig deep underground, dive underwater, and even search through ice-covered terrain to uncover anything from tiny hidden treasures to entire ancient skeletons. The most interesting and exciting of these finds end up in museums around the world so that visitors can experience them and learn more about them.

ARCHAEOLOGIST

Archaeologists study historical sites around the world by removing layers of earth and sand to reveal what's underneath. They uncover buried objects and the ruins of structures such as houses and monuments. These objects and structures provide exciting evidence about our ancestors. As they dig, archaeologists make drawings, write notes, and take photographs to record information about the exact location and condition of the objects and ruins they find.

Metal tools are used to scrape earth from artifacts.

Archaeologist's toolkit

Excavation can be hard physical work, but it mostly requires precision. An archaeologist's toolkit includes small trowels and narrow brushes to carefully remove earth from precious artifacts.

▲ Burial site
In Peru, an archaeologist works to uncover human remains, ceramics, and textiles in a burial site from 1000–1450 BCE.

Underground ruins cause vegetation to dry out at different rates, creating outlines of old buildings.

Aerial archaeology

Before digging, archaeologists research potential historical sites. They study historical documents and old maps, but one of the best ways to assess an area is from above. They look at images taken by satellites or drones to search for ruins. During the summer of 2018, a long heat wave in the England exposed ancient imprints. As the soil dried out, lines, known as crop marks, appeared in the soil. In this field in Devon, England, these crop marks are thought to show where a Roman settlement once stood.

TERRA-COTTA ARMY

In 246 BCE, Chinese Emperor Qin Shi Huang ordered the creation of an army of terra-cotta (baked clay) soldiers to guard his underground tomb after he died. More than 700,000 laborers worked on this enormous army until construction stopped two years after the emperor's death in 210 BCE. Emperor Qin's sculptures were forgotten about for more than 2,000 years. But in 1974, while digging a well near the city of Xi'an, China, a group of farmers stumbled across one of the greatest ever archaeological discoveries.

An emperor's army

Before it was buried in earth, Emperor Qin's terra-cotta army had been arranged in rows, just like a real army ready for battle. Archaeologists think there are more than 8,000 soldiers, 130 chariots, and 670 horses in the pits.

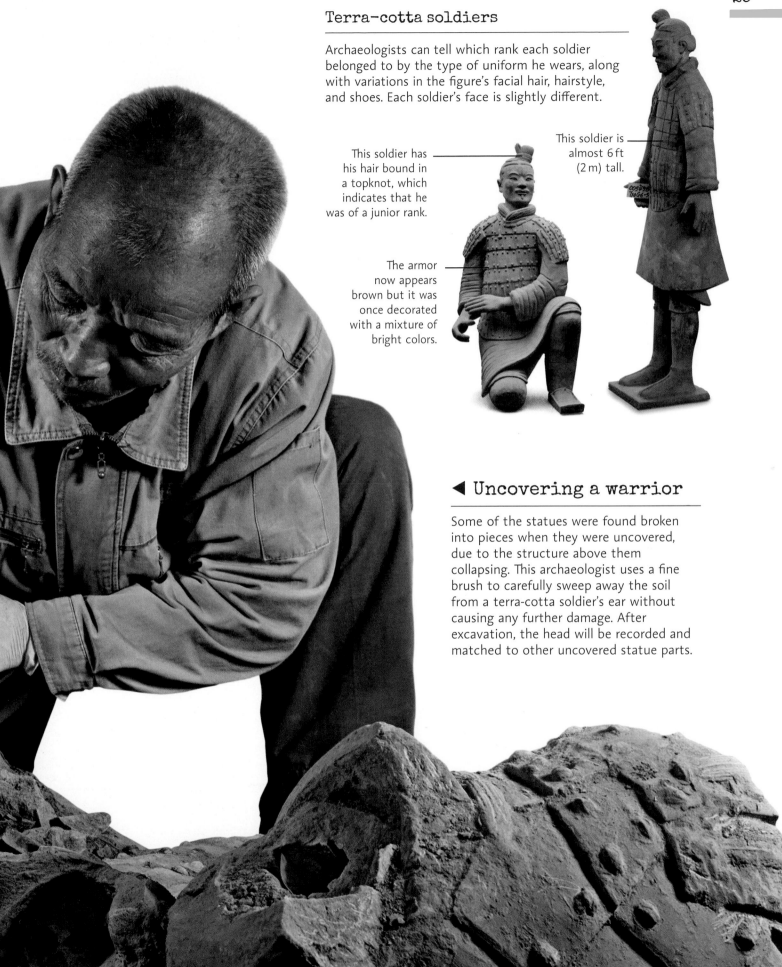

Terra-cotta soldiers

Archaeologists can tell which rank each soldier belonged to by the type of uniform he wears, along with variations in the figure's facial hair, hairstyle, and shoes. Each soldier's face is slightly different.

This soldier has his hair bound in a topknot, which indicates that he was of a junior rank.

This soldier is almost 6 ft (2 m) tall.

The armor now appears brown but it was once decorated with a mixture of bright colors.

◀ Uncovering a warrior

Some of the statues were found broken into pieces when they were uncovered, due to the structure above them collapsing. This archaeologist uses a fine brush to carefully sweep away the soil from a terra-cotta soldier's ear without causing any further damage. After excavation, the head will be recorded and matched to other uncovered statue parts.

BURIAL SITE UNCOVERED

Emperor Qin's burial site covered an area of more than 22 square miles (57 square kilometers). Archaeologists still haven't completed excavating the whole site, but so far they've dug almost 600 pits, each 23 ft (7 m) deep. Not all of the statues in the pits were discovered whole—in this photograph is a pile of broken terra-cotta fragments waiting to be sorted. The archaeologists have installed lights and ladders to help their work. Sandbags on top of the pit walls prevent loose soil from falling into the space below.

Repairing the soldiers

While some archaeologists remove earth from the pits, others record, clean, and painstakingly piece the fragments of terra-cotta to rebuild the statues as they appeared originally.

Fragile pieces
Archaeologists reconstruct a headless torso from broken fragments. Some pieces are as small as fingernails.

Complete soldiers
Once rebuilt, the soldiers are placed neatly in rows, positioned just as they were when they were first arranged in Emperor Qin's burial site more than 2,000 years ago.

FROZEN HORSES

In the frosty landscapes of Norway, many ancient artifacts lie hidden in the ice. When the ice melts during warmer weather, which now happens more regularly due to climate change, artifacts are sometimes found lying on the ground, often well preserved thanks to the sub-zero temperatures of past centuries. A team of Norwegian archaeologists, known as "Secrets of the Ice," search the thawing landscape for artifacts. Since 2006, they have found more than 3,000 items, from tools to clothing.

► Bones on the ice

Between 300 and 1700, people and their horses regularly traveled across the Lendbreen ice patch in Norway. Archaeologists have since found many artifacts frozen in the ice here. This archaeologist is collecting the rib bones of a horse that died while crossing the ice patch. The freezing temperatures helped preserve its bones.

Horse skull
Archaeologists found this horse skull at the Lendbreen ice patch in Norway. The horse died around 300 years ago while traveling with humans, carrying loads for them.

Icy discovery

In 2019, the Secrets of the Ice team discovered an exceptionally well-preserved snowshoe, thought to be from the late medieval period, between 1250 and 1500. Snowshoes would have been attached by travelers to horses' hooves to help them trudge through the icy terrain.

Found in the ice
Recent snowfall on the snowshoe itself had melted quicker than the snow around it, making it visible on the ground.

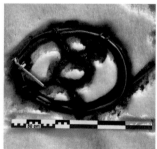

Measuring as found
The snowshoe was measured. Its condition suggested that it had long been frozen in solid ice before it was discovered.

Collecting the shoe
A team member carefully removed the snowshoe from the ice before taking it to a lab for further study.

SUNKEN SECRETS

Maritime archaeologists study historical sites in lakes, rivers, and oceans. They look underwater for shipwrecks, crashed aircraft, and ancient settlements flooded by rising sea levels. Many factors affect how well an artifact survives underwater, such as how salty the water is, how strong the currents are, and whether sea creatures have eaten away at the artifact. After assessing an artifact's condition, maritime archaeologists must decide whether or not it is stable enough to be raised to the surface.

▶ Underwater excavation

In 2012, a team of maritime archaeologists surveyed an ancient shipwreck off the coast of the Greek island of Antikythera. The ship sank in around 60 BCE. It was first discovered in 1900 when artifacts including bronze statues and marble sculptures were recovered. During the 2012 dive, the maritime archaeologists, two of whom are shown working here, found many more artifacts, including pottery, weapons, and even a human skeleton.

Cranks and gears cause the needles to move into place.

The Antikythera Mechanism

Dating back to the 2nd century BCE, this "ancient computer" is the most famous artifact discovered in the Antikythera shipwreck. An incredibly sophisticated machine for its time, it has dials that experts think were used to track the phases of the Moon and even predict solar and lunar eclipses.

Underwater tasks

Many of the archaeological processes carried out underwater are the same as those used on land. Maritime archaeologists make notes about artifacts, create maps, and take photographs.

Documenting artifacts
Divers make notes about artifacts and draw detailed maps using waterproof pens and whiteboards.

Making a grid
Divers set up string grids to mark areas into squares. These squares allow them to precisely record the location of any objects found during an excavation.

Uncovering artifacts
Divers can't use trowels to excavate buried artifacts as they would create clouds of dust. Instead, they use vacuums to suck up the sand around an object.

FLOODED CITY

This enormous statue was part of the ancient seaport of Thonis-Heracleion, which was submerged during the 2nd century BCE after different natural catastrophes caused the city to sink. After more than 2,000 years at the bottom of the sea, the red granite statue of the ancient Egyptian god Hapi was winched to the surface by maritime archaeologist Franck Goddio and his team off the coast of Alexandria in Egypt. It is one of hundreds of artifacts raised between 1996 and the present day.

Back on dry land

The statue weighs 12,000 lb (6 metric tons) and is almost 18 ft (5.5 m) high. According to ancient Egyptian beliefs, Hapi was the god of the yearly flooding of the Nile. The statue is now on display at the National Maritime Museum in Alexandria, Egypt.

▼ Island statue

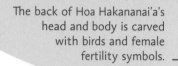

To the people of Rapa Nui, this sacred statue, known as Hoa Hakananai'a ("stolen friend"), is an important ancestor figure (moai) inhabited by protective spirits. The 8-ft- (2.5-m-) high statue was carried away by the crew of a British warship in 1868 and given to Queen Victoria.

The back of Hoa Hakananai'a's head and body is carved with birds and female fertility symbols.

THE BACK OF HOA HAKANANAI'A

ANCIENT STATUES

Although many museum artifacts are collected, bought, or donated, some were in fact taken against the wishes of indigenous communities. Many of the historical artifacts on Rapa Nui (Easter Island) in the Pacific Ocean were removed by European explorers, including figures, axes, and other objects, and placed in museum collections around the world. The people of Rapa Nui have been seeking the return of these items, leading to much debate.

Carved heads

Approximately 887 stone sculptures (moai) once stood on Easter Island. Most were sculpted between 1100 and 1600. They were carved from soft volcanic stone or basalt, and painted with red and white designs. Their eyes were inlaid with coral and red stone. Standing on specially built platforms, they faced inland.

Ownership debate

The statue is currently at the British Museum in London, England. Many people have called for it to be returned to Rapa Nui due to its spiritual and historical importance. Others argue that it receives world-class care at the British Museum and acts as an ambassador of Rapa Nui culture to millions of people. The British Museum has agreed to discuss the statue's future with the people of Rapa Nui.

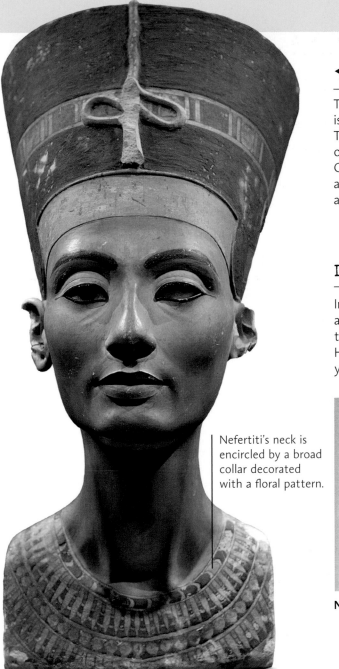

Nefertiti's neck is encircled by a broad collar decorated with a floral pattern.

◀ Queen Nefertiti

This bust of the 18th-dynasty Egyptian Queen Nefertiti is thought to have been created in around 1340 BCE. The life-size sculpture was carved from a single block of limestone and weighs 44 lb (20 kg). It was taken to Germany in 1913 by the archaeologist Ludwig Borchardt, and remains on display at Berlin's Neues Museum, although Egypt has requested its return.

Ludwig Borchardt

In this note from 1912, Ludwig Borchardt expresses joy at his discovery of the sculpture of Nefertiti, describing the ribboned wig and the fresh appearance of the paint. He writes: "Really wonderful work. No use describing it, you have to see it."

NOTE FROM LUDWIG BORCHARDT

Borchardt's sketch of the bust includes a measurement of its height as 18½ in (47 cm).

Perfect replicas

The bust of Nefertiti is one of the most copied artifacts from ancient Egypt. Using today's modern techniques, specialists can produce incredibly accurate replicas. Even an item's imperfections or signs of damage are reproduced, making the copy indistinguishable from the original. High-quality replicas mean that more people around the world can marvel at famous artifacts without having to move the valuable, often fragile, originals.

THE BENIN BRONZES

The Benin Bronzes are a huge collection of plaques and sculptures, most of which date back to the 16th century. They were crafted in the Kingdom of Benin, located in present-day Nigeria, which ruled from the late 12th century until 1897 when a British military expedition captured Benin City and exiled the Oba (king). British troops looted the palace and thousands of brass, wood, ivory, and coral artworks were taken out of Nigeria. Many pieces ended up in private collections and public museums in Europe and the US. More than a century later, the British Museum in London, England, is preparing to lend some of the objects in its care to a new Royal Museum in Benin City, Nigeria.

▶ The Benin plaques

The Benin plaques, of which there are more than 1,000, originally decorated the wooden columns in the royal palace of the Kingdom of Benin. They featured nobles, warriors, and royals, and recorded everyday and court life in the palace. On this plaque, the Oba of Benin is shown with four royal attendants.

This brass head with iron inlaid eyes is believed to represent the 16th-century Queen Mother Idia.

Memorial heads

These memorial heads would have been placed on altars dedicated to recently deceased royals. Memorial heads were commissioned by the crown prince, the son of the Oba.

ON DISPLAY

Columns of plaques
Some of the Benin Bronzes are on display at the British Museum in London, as shown here. There are large collections in Germany and the US, too.

Disputed ownership

In 1897, Britain was in the process of strengthening its imperial control of southern Nigeria. In response to the Oba's resistance, the British military launched an expedition to capture Benin, the Kingdom of Benin's capital city. The Oba was exiled. The royal palace and its treasures were looted. Controversially, they have largely remained in European and US collections ever since they were taken.

Holes through the top and bottom of the plaque were made for nails, which secured it to a wooden column in the palace.

A royal attendant flanks the Oba, protecting the king's head with a raised shield.

The attendant's elaborately patterned cloth shows his status. Young servants within the court, known as "emada", are generally represented as unclothed.

XXIV, 5.

98
I -15.
38

These Roman numerals represent the number assigned to the plaque by staff at the British Museum in the 1899 Read & Dalton catalogue.

BIG MUSEUMS

Some of the world's biggest museums grew out of royal collections (which were originally ways of displaying wealth and power); others were established to showcase a country's national history. These grand museums house rare and extraordinary objects from around the world, giving visitors intriguing snapshots of human history.

SMITHSONIAN INSTITUTION

Washington, D.C., is home to the largest museum complex in the world—the Smithsonian. It includes 19 museums that look after a mind-boggling 155.5 million items.

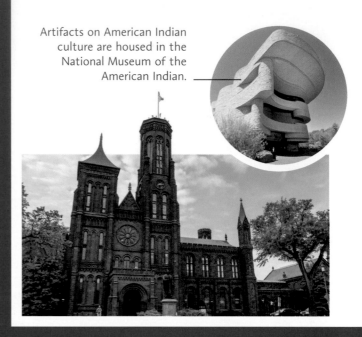

Artifacts on American Indian culture are housed in the National Museum of the American Indian.

The design of the front of the British Museum building was inspired by ancient Greek temples.

THE BRITISH MUSEUM

Established in 1753, the British Museum in London, England, was the world's first national museum. It houses items that provide a fascinating history of culture and art around the world.

8,000,000

The number of objects in the collection.

THE NATIONAL MUSEUM OF CHINA

There are 48 exhibition halls in China's national museum in Beijing. On display are precious treasures from the ancient world, such as burial suits threaded with gold, a pillow made from jade, and the largest piece of bronzeware in the world, the Houmuwu Ding, a sacred vessel.

The Houmuwu Ding is decorated with real and mythological creatures.

THE LOUVRE

The Louvre in Paris, France, is the largest art museum in the world, though it has many historical artifacts, too. Among its priceless collection is Leonardo da Vinci's *Mona Lisa*, which once hung on Napoleon's bedroom wall.

35,000
The number of artworks in the museum.

THE VATICAN MUSEUMS

The Vatican Museums in Rome, Italy, grew to house the fabulous collections gathered by various popes. Altogether, there are 54 museums, and if you visit each one, be prepared to walk 4 miles (7 km). Highlights include the magnificent ceiling of the Sistine Chapel, which took the Italian artist Michelangelo four years to paint.

THE HERMITAGE

Originally started by Empress Catherine the Great in 1764, Russia's state museum in Saint Petersburg today houses a collection of 3 million objects. It also includes historic buildings such as the Winter Palace, which was once the home of Russian emperors.

This life-size golden peacock is part of a clock that belonged to Catherine the Great.

BEST OF THE REST

▶ NATIONAL MUSEUM OF ANTHROPOLOGY

Mexico's national museum in Mexico City houses the world's largest collection of ancient Mexican art.

▶ TOKYO NATIONAL MUSEUM

Japan's national museum houses an important treasure-trove of Japanese art and archaeology as well as Asian art.

▶ NATIONAL MUSEUM OF KOREA

About 300,000 priceless artifacts are housed in Korea's vast national museum in Seoul, showcasing the country's history and culture.

A MAMMOTH TASK

In 2006, a group of construction workers digging near La Brea Tar Pits located in Los Angeles, California, US, stumbled upon a discovery. Buried in the tar were around 700 bones from animals such as ancient lions and sabre-toothed cats. They also found a nearly complete skeleton of an adult Columbian mammoth (which became known as Zed). These fossils were all preserved when the tar trapped the animals over a period of 10,000 to 40,000 years ago.

▶ Plaster-cast bones
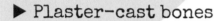

Fossilized tusks and bones are very fragile. When excavators moved some specimens to the museum at La Brea Tar Pits, they encased them in plaster to keep them safe—just like a plaster cast for a broken bone. This preserved the fine physical details of the specimens, as well as their shape and size.

A wooden support holds the 10-ft- (3-m-) long tusk securely in place.

Sharp tools are used to remove the outer layers of plaster cast.

Excavation site

The site was so full of fossils that instead of excavating them all there and then, the team decided to lift away entire sections of earth, boxing them directly into 23 large wooden crates to be excavated later above ground. But due to Zed's size, the earth around his skeleton had to be sifted away and the remains removed separately.

Giant pelvis

Zed's skeleton was particularly important to paleontologists because it was around 80 percent complete when they discovered it, making it one of the most complete mammoth skeletons ever found. Here, a pair of volunteers are cleaning dirt off his massive pelvis bone. Zed would have been a large mammoth—around 10 ft (3 m) tall at the hip. Studies of Zed's bones reveal that he was between 47 and 49 years old when he died.

DID YOU KNOW?

Columbian mammoths could weigh 20,000 lb (10 metric tons). The species became extinct 11,500 years ago.

A lab supervisor begins the delicate work of cleaning Zed's left tusk.

A section of the plaster jacket has been removed.

SPECIMEN HUNTERS

Natural history museums often have large collections of dead animal specimens. In the past, huge numbers of wild animals were killed so they could be studied and displayed in museums. Although this practice still takes place today, it happens on a much smaller scale, only when deemed necessary, and always with animal conservation in mind.

Lifelike illustrations

Before photography and video were invented, the only way for many people to see or study certain animals was using dead specimens. However, some artists produced anatomically correct artworks, like this illustration of a fish by Ferdinand Bauer (1760–1826), which could be used instead of capturing and killing wild animals.

Finding animals

There was a time when explorers collected anything and everything that they could find. In March 1909, museum workers from the Smithsonian Institution and former US President Theodore Roosevelt went on a hunting expedition to Africa. While there, they collected approximately 11,400 animal specimens, including 5,000 skins of mammals, in addition to 10,000 plant specimens.

The smaller, sharper beaks were best for catching small insects.

Labels were tagged to each specimen's legs.

Handwritten labels note the species and the specimen number.

▼ Darwin's finches

Darwin collected many animal specimens during his travels aboard the HMS *Beagle* between 1831 and 1836. These finches from the Galapagos Islands, whose beak formations are thought to have fueled Darwin's theories of evolution, are perhaps his best-known finds and are still held by the Natural History Museum in London, England, today.

Larger beaks were better adapted to eating seeds from the ground.

In the sewers

London's sewers date back to the 1850s, and they sometimes have problems dealing with 21st-century life. The fatberg is the perfect example of how these sewers sometimes struggle to cope.

Blocked tunnel
Cooking fat poured down the drain, combined with other waste materials, formed a giant fatberg that built up in the sewer over time. When found, it was more than twice the length of a soccer field.

Entering the sewers
Specialists went down into the sewer to break the fatberg into smaller pieces. These could then be brought to the surface through pipes.

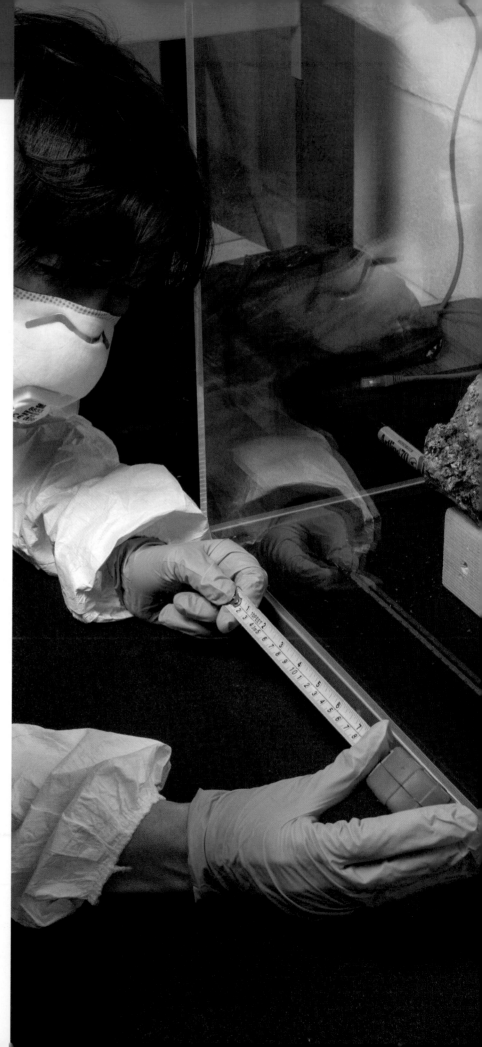

GIANT
FATBERG

In 2017, an enormous mass of cooking fat, wet wipes, human waste, and other trash was discovered in the sewers underneath London, England. This monstrous "fatberg" was blocking the sewers and needed to be removed quickly. But the Museum of London saw this blockage as more than just smelly sewage—they saw an opportunity to put something truly unique on display.

◀ First of its kind

When the Museum of London decided to conserve small pieces of the fatberg, they had no examples to follow—no other museum in the world had tried to do this before. After testing its chemical makeup, they decided to air-dry it to remove any destructive moisture. They recorded it 24 hours a day, by video camera, to see exactly what changes took place as the pieces dried—they changed color and even hatched flies! Before being put on display, the fatberg was placed inside three layers of protective casing to ensure the public was protected from any diseases it contained.

Hazmat display

To venture into the sewer, the crew removing the fatberg had to wear hazmat suits to protect themselves from any dangerous diseases that thrived within it.

3

SORTING
THE PAST

Museums are home to collections of thousands, sometimes even millions, of artifacts and specimens that document the history of people and the planet, from ancient fossils to new technologies. Without proper organization, it would be easy for these artifacts to go missing, get damaged, or even cause people harm. Whether it's assessing the condition of new items coming into the collection, securing a priceless diamond from theft, or even safely storing a radioactive notebook, museums have a responsibility to look after the objects in their care for future generations.

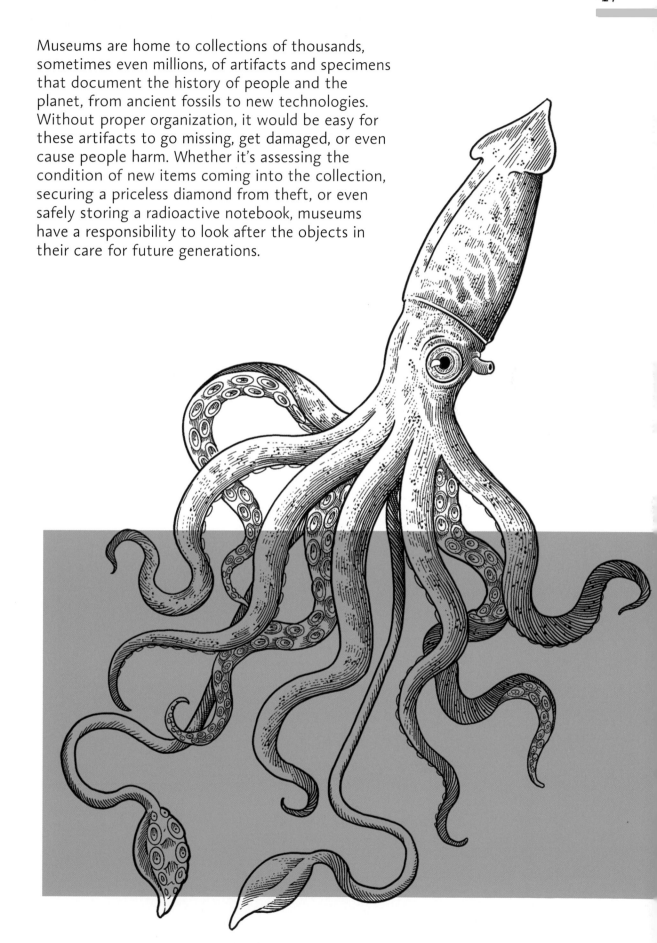

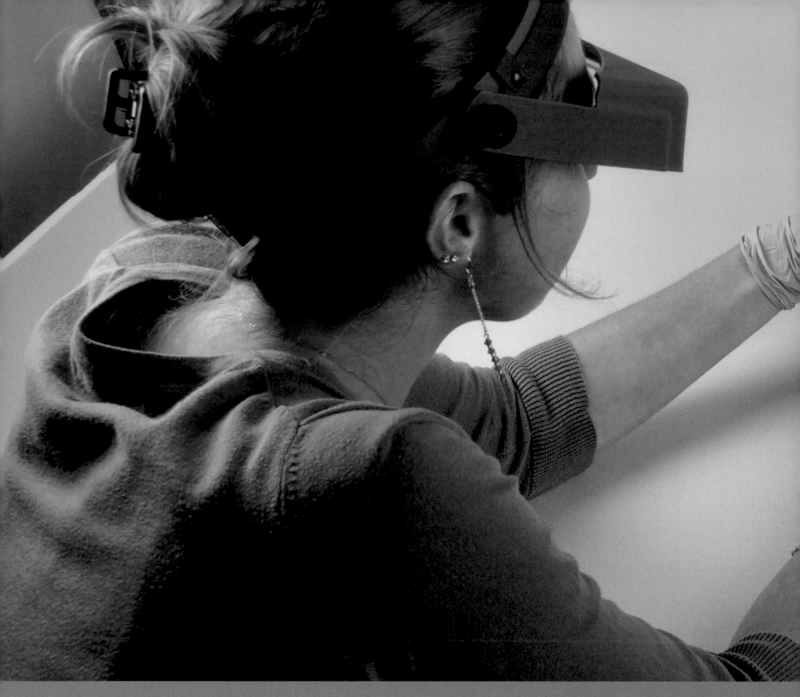

ROLES BEHIND THE SCENES
REGISTRAR

A registrar is responsible for keeping track of the whereabouts of all the objects in a museum. Whenever an object is moved—either within a museum or loaned to another museum—it is documented by the registrar. Even small museums can hold tens of thousands of objects, so registrars must be very organized. When objects are moved, registrars often take photographs of them and check their condition, to see whether they have been damaged. They are then placed in storage, or passed onto conservators for treatment.

Magnification goggles
When inspecting the condition of an object, registrars often wear a pair of magnification goggles, so that they can see it clearly in minute detail.

▲ Condition report
This registrar at the Penn Museum is inspecting a small figurine from Khafaje, Iraq, in order to write a report on its current condition.

Engineers used special carts that blew jets of air under the statue. This made it hover a couple inches off the ground, making it easier to move.

Transporting artifacts

When artifacts are moved, registrars often accompany them in person to make sure that they stay safe. This enormous sphinx was moved 250 ft (76 m) along a carefully planned route from one gallery to another within the Musée des Confluences in Lyon.

LABELED SPECIMENS

Every specimen and artifact in a museum should be labeled, to make sure that registrars can keep track of it. With some museums having millions of specimens in their collections, it might be years before that item is found again. Writing labels and cataloging items is extremely important as, if done incorrectly, a conservator might put an item back in the wrong place. These bees have tiny labels that record the species they are. There are around 20,000 species of bee in the world.

Labeling fossils

With up to 10,000 new specimens arriving annually, the National Museums of Kenya's paleontology department has a constant backlog of fossils to clean, catalog, and label. The department's 15 staff members have tons of material to analyze. Fossils are labeled with information about their formation, their age, and where they were found, as well as an identification number.

CARBON DATING

When an ancient artifact is discovered, one of the first things archaeologists want to find out is just how old it is. For many years, they relied on techniques to date an object based on factors such as how far underground it was found or, for a human-made artifact, the way it was made. Today, these techniques are still used, but many scientists now regularly use a more accurate method known as carbon dating, which can give a much more precise estimate of an artifact's age.

▶ Age estimation

All living things absorb carbon-14, a radioactive form of the element carbon found in the atmosphere. When they die, the carbon-14 in their bodies starts to break down at a regular, known rate. When archaeologists discover plant and animal remains (such as the human leg bone in this image), they take a sample and run tests on it to measure how much carbon-14 is left. The less carbon-14 they find in the object, the older it is.

The Tarkhan dress

Unearthed from an ancient Egyptian tomb in 1913, this linen garment lay undiscovered in a pile of textiles until 1977 when it was sent to the Victoria and Albert Museum in London, England. Carbon dating showed that the dress was made sometime between 3482 and 3102 BCE, making it the oldest piece of woven clothing ever discovered. It is now on display at the UCL Petrie Museum of Egyptian Archaeology in London, England.

Museum laboratory

Carbon dating requires a large, expensive machine called an accelerator mass spectrometer. Very few laboratories have the specialized equipment needed to carry out this complicated process.

Drilling a hole
Here, the scientist carefully drills a small hole in a human leg bone from medieval times. She removes a tiny sample for analysis.

Preparing the sample
The sample is placed in a vial. It must be kept completely pure—even a tiny amount of contamination could make the result inaccurate by tens of thousands of years.

Carbon dating machine
The sample is put into the spectrometer and vaporized. As millions of the sample's atoms scatter, the machine calculates how many of them are carbon-14 by measuring their speed. The amount of carbon-14 indicates the bone's age.

HUMAN REMAINS

Many museum collections contain human bodies, skeletons, and mummified remains. There is often little information about how these human remains came to be in museums, but they help scientists and historians carry out research into the past. Museum workers handle human remains carefully, treating them with respect. However, some communities still question whether they should be stored or displayed in museums at all. Instead, some people think all human remains should be returned to their communities of origin for reburial.

▶ Bodies in storage

Mexico's National Museum of Anthropology is more than a collection of artifacts. Few of its 2 million yearly visitors know that its basement contains more than 25,000 human bones in carefully organized boxes, as well as 30 mummies. There are also 51 skeletons dating from before 2000 BCE—the oldest of which is 12,700 years old.

Mummified bundles, Peru

Before the 16th century, the Chachapoyas people of Peru buried their dead in remote locations. The bones of the deceased were dried and bound in cloth together with plants and ceremonial offerings for the afterlife. Many were taken from burial sites, eventually ending up in private and public collections worldwide. These mummified bundles are kept at the Leymebamba Museum in Peru.

Research specimens

Human remains can serve a variety of research functions. Fossilized skull specimens, for example, let researchers find out the brain size of early human populations. Here, this skull specimen is being filled with grains. The grains are then poured into a vessel to measure their volume. The volume of grains will reveal the skull's brain size.

CHOLULA PUEBLA
UNIDAD21K-39Z
1968
ENT. 297
236
CHOLULA PUEBLA
UNIDAD21K-42X
1969
ENT-323
254
CHOLULA PUEBLA
UNIDAD21K-14U
1968
217
CHOLULA PUEBLA
UNIDAD21K-41D
218
CHOLULA PUEBLA
UNIDAD21K-40Y
1968
237
CHOLULA PUEBLA
UNIDAD21K-43Z
1969
ENT.327
256
ENT. 372
CHOLULA PUEBLA
UNIDAD21K-10U
1968
219
CHOLULA PUEBLA
UNIDAD21K-39Y
1968
ENTS.299-300
238
CHOLULA PUEBLA
UNIDAD20L-1 A
1969
ENTS.328-329
257
ENT-370
CHOLULA PUEBLA
UNIDAD 21K-10T
1968
220
CHOLULA PUEBLA
UNIDAD21K-40Z
1968
ENT.301
239
CHOLULA PUEBLA
UNIDAD20L-1A
1969
ENTS. 330-331
258
ENT. 372
CHOLULA PUEBLA
UNIDAD21K-40F
1968
221
CHOLULA PUEBLA
UNIDAD21K-39Z
1968
ENT. 302
240
CHOLULA PUEBLA
UNIDAD20L-1A
1969
ENTS. 332-333
259
ENTS. 372
REMINGTON
110
111
PUEBLA
UNIDAD
1968
222
CHOLULA
1968
ENTS-303-304
260
CHOLULA PUEBLA
UNIDAD 21L-25N-21K
40D 1968
223
CHOLULA PUEBLA
UNIDAD21K-27K
1969
ENTS.338-339-340
261
UNIDAD21K-40F
1968
224
UNIDAD21K-12M
ENTS-341-342
262
UNIDAD21K-40G
1968
225
UNIDAD21K-40G
1968
UNIDAD21K-14U

Sixteen white diamonds, shaped like squares or pears, surround the blue diamond in the middle.

The Hope Diamond is very light— it only weighs about ⅓ oz (9 g) and is roughly the size of a walnut.

THE HOPE DIAMOND

Few jewels have as unusual a past as the Hope Diamond—it is one of the best-known precious gems in the world. Famous for its ocean-blue coloring, the gem is thought by some to carry a sinister curse that brings tragedy to all who touch it. It has a long history of famous owners, including King Louis XIV of France.

▲ The Hope Diamond

Originally discovered in India in the 17th century, the Hope Diamond is unusual because most diamonds appear clear. It is one of the largest known blue diamonds in the world. The jewel is currently set in a dazzling necklace, designed by French jeweler Pierre Cartier. It was placed in the middle of the pendant in 1912 and is surrounded by a ring of white diamonds.

The chain of the necklace contains 45 white diamonds.

The packaging used to send the diamond is on display at the Smithsonian's National Postal Museum.

The color blue

In 2009, scientists at the Smithsonian's mineralogy lab borrowed the Hope Diamond for a day to find out exactly what makes it so blue.

The team put the diamond into a machine called a mass spectrometer to find out what elements the diamond contained. Diamonds are mostly made of carbon, but may contain other elements, too.

They used the machine to fire an ion beam at the gem. This made a hole, just four-billionths of an inch in size, in the diamond, and sent millions of its atoms flying into the machine for analysis.

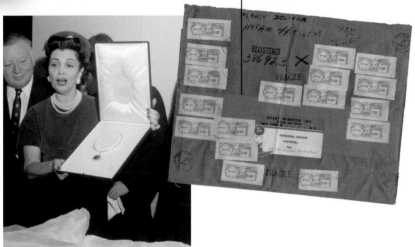

Diamond donation

In 1958, after owning it for 11 years, American jeweler Harry Winston donated the Hope Diamond to the Smithsonian, where it is now one of the museum's most famous artifacts. He sent the gem from his store in New York to the museum in Washington, D.C., by mail—a surprising delivery method for one of the most famous diamonds in the world. It cost him $2.44 (£1.87) to mail the parcel and he paid $142.85 (£109.57) to insure it for up to $1 million (£767,000).

The scientists found that, as well as carbon, hydrogen, and perhaps nitrogen, the Hope Diamond contains varying amounts of boron throughout the jewel, creating different shades of blue.

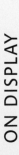

ON DISPLAY

Secure conditions
The diamond is the main attraction and centerpiece of the Smithsonian National Gem Collection at the National Museum of Natural History in Washington, D.C. It is on display in a secure case surrounded by bulletproof glass, and is placed on a rotating pedestal so it can be viewed from all angles.

LAB ON DISPLAY

Following its huge renovation, the Hall of Fossils at the Smithsonian National Museum of Natural History in Washington, D.C., reopened in 2019. It unveiled a new permanent exhibit, *Deep Time*. As well as displaying ancient and prehistoric fossils that tell the history of Earth, curators wanted to share with museum visitors how these fossils are prepared, studied, and conserved. They created FossiLab to give visitors the chance to peer into a real working museum laboratory and get a glimpse of the work that usually goes on behind the scenes.

▶ Volunteer at work

FossiLab is a unique opportunity for visitors to see experts at work. This volunteer is using a microscope to inspect loose sediment from a dig site, searching for tiny fossils of ancient animals such as frogs, lizards, fish, and mammals. The microscope's view is shown on a small screen so visitors can see exactly what's happening.

Department on show

FossiLab has become a very popular exhibit, with crowds gathering around the large glass windows. Visitors are intrigued by the big blue tubes that help to remove dust from the air, and the large storage boxes full of red sand used to support fragile fossils as they are worked on. The sand is actually crushed garnet (a red gemstone). Unlike beach sand, garnet does not contain silica dust, which would harm the volunteers' lungs over time.

DID YOU KNOW?

Some small fossils can be prepared for display in just an hour, but large ones can take years of work before they're ready.

FossiLab tasks

FossiLab is staffed by a team of highly trained volunteers who work on fossils fresh from dig sites. They carry out specialized tasks to prepare these fossils ready for research or display.

Recording the specimens
A volunteer skilfully and accurately draws a fossil jaw. Scientific illustrations record the important features of fossils and can be easier to understand than photographs.

Preparing to display
A volunteer and curator talk about a fossil palm frond that has been prepared for display. To prepare the fossil, the volunteer removed a layer of rock that was covering it.

X-RAY VISION

Some museum exhibits contain hidden mysteries, such as other objects trapped inside them. Breaking open a rare or precious exhibit to reveal its insides would damage it, so instead researchers use machines called CT scanners to see inside.

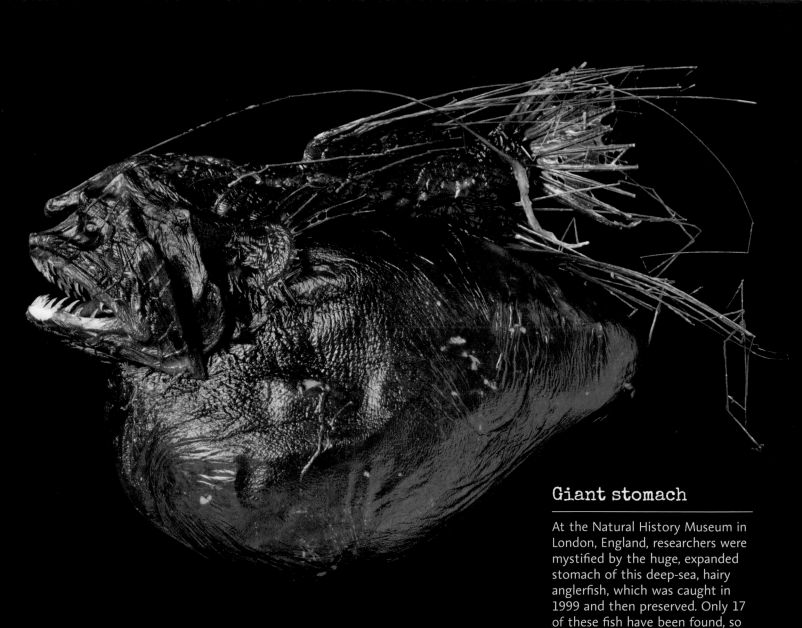

Giant stomach

At the Natural History Museum in London, England, researchers were mystified by the huge, expanded stomach of this deep-sea, hairy anglerfish, which was caught in 1999 and then preserved. Only 17 of these fish have been found, so scientists didn't want to cut open the rare specimen. Instead, they used a CT scanner to look inside.

Scanning fossils

Even fossils can be scanned to see inside. This scientist used a special kind of CT scanner to produce a beam of X-rays 100 billion times more powerful than a medical X-ray machine. Before the main scan, a green laser beam, shown here, was used to position the specimen—the fossil of an ammonite (a prehistoric sea creature). The final scan revealed microscopic details inside the ammonite.

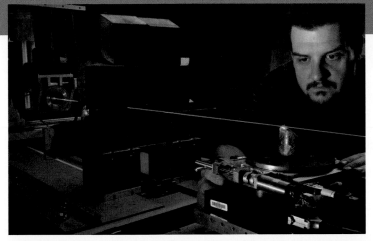

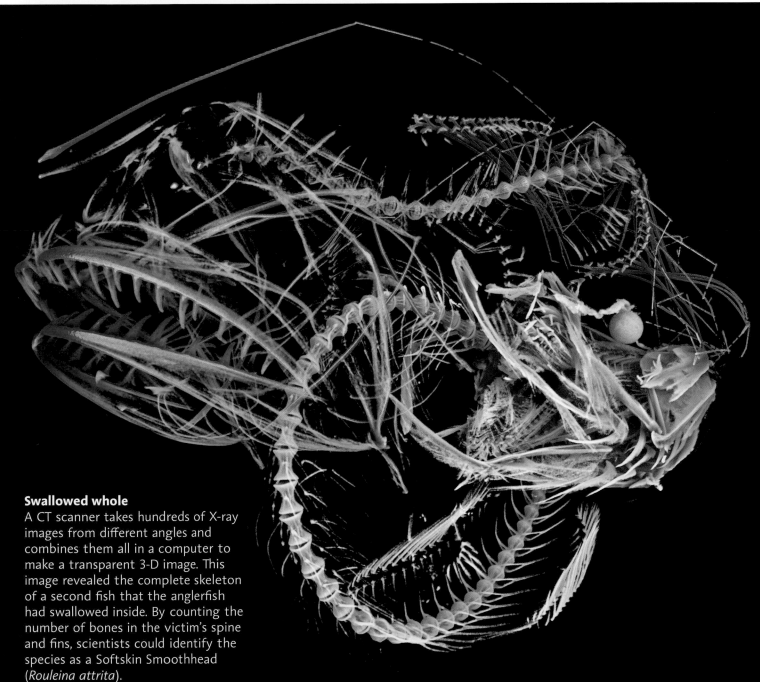

Swallowed whole
A CT scanner takes hundreds of X-ray images from different angles and combines them all in a computer to make a transparent 3-D image. This image revealed the complete skeleton of a second fish that the anglerfish had swallowed inside. By counting the number of bones in the victim's spine and fins, scientists could identify the species as a Softskin Smoothhead (*Rouleina attrita*).

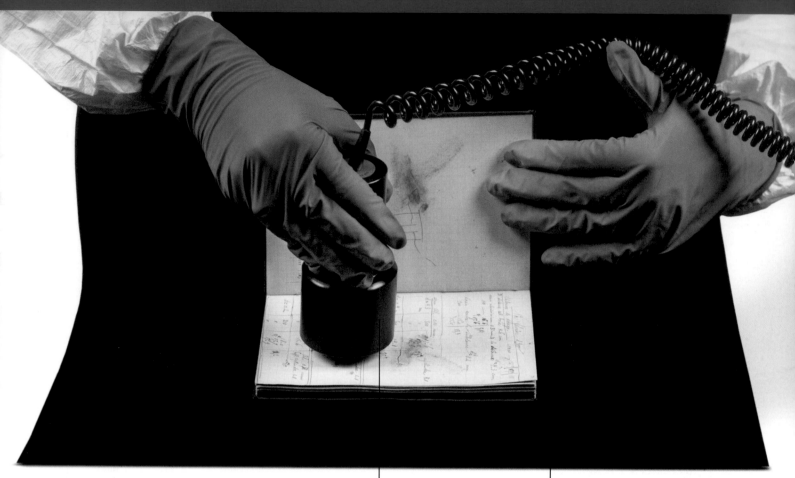

▲ Safety precautions

If library staff want to examine Marie Curie's notebooks, they must sign a document accepting the risks and wear protective clothing such as gloves.

A Geiger counter is a machine that detects ionizing radiation (harmful particles released by atoms).

This black shield absorbs radiation that could otherwise cause harm.

MARIE CURIE'S NOTEBOOKS

Marie Curie (1867–1934) was a research scientist. She discovered the radioactive elements radium and polonium, for which she became the first person to be awarded Nobel Prizes in both physics and chemistry. She died from a rare condition caused by exposure to high levels of radiation. Her handwritten notebooks are still contaminated with the radioactive element radium 226, posing a challenge for library staff at the Bibliothèque nationale in Paris, France, where the notebooks are stored.

The Geiger counter's display shows the amount of radiation currently being emitted by the notebook.

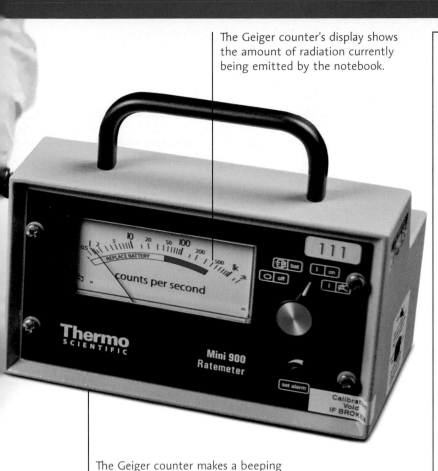

The Geiger counter makes a beeping sound when it detects radiation.

Warning sign

The radiation warning symbols on the notebooks' protective casing alert library staff to the health risks of handling them. Without the correct protection, they could be at risk of radiation poisoning.

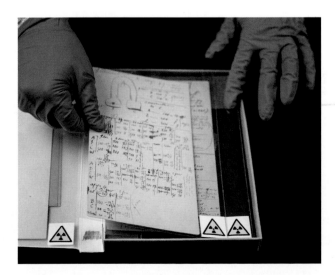

Dangerous artifacts

Museum artifacts can pose a risk to staff, visitors, and even to the objects themselves. Most museums regularly assess the items in their collections for whether or not they are dangerous.

Poisonous weapons
Some weapons are tested for traces of toxic substances from poisons that can remain effective for up to 1,500 years.

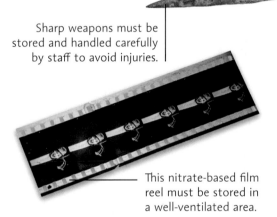

Sharp weapons must be stored and handled carefully by staff to avoid injuries.

This nitrate-based film reel must be stored in a well-ventilated area.

Film reels
Between 1910 and 1950, it was popular for movies to be made using nitrate-based film reels. These reels release gases, which can build up if the reels are stored in closed containers, making them highly explosive.

This dress was dyed using arsenic, a highly toxic chemical.

Arsenic-based dyes
In the 19th century, green clothes were fashionable, despite the fact that some green dyes were made from arsenic— a toxic chemical that caused harm to the garment makers using them. Today, museum workers must wear gloves when handling items colored with arsenic-based dyes.

MESSAGES IN BOTTLES

Biologists often use animal specimens held in museums to study different species from around the world. Museums sometimes preserve these specimens in jars, to keep them in good condition so that they can be studied. The Natural History Museum in London, England, has one of the world's biggest collections, with 17 miles (27 km) of shelves filled with jarred, or "wet," specimens, including some that were collected by English scientist Charles Darwin during the 1830s.

▼ Wet specimens

To make a wet specimen, a conservator first injects the dead animal with a liquid chemical that preserves and hardens the organs inside its body. They then place the specimen into a jar, submerging it in more preservative chemicals, which help it retain a lifelike appearance.

DID YOU KNOW?

The Natural History Museum in London has more than 22 million wet specimens in its collection.

The Natural History Museum's specimen jars are windows to the work of earlier scientists.

The jars are sealed with air-tight lids to further protect the specimens from decay.

Giant specimens

One of the world's largest animals to be preserved as a wet specimen is a giant squid (*Architeuthis dux*). Known as "Archie," the squid is 28 ft (8.5 m) long and kept in a custom-made tank at the Natural History Museum. Conservators froze the squid after it was caught in 2004, while an enormous tank was built to store the specimen. They then injected it with formalsaline (a mixture of salt water and formaldehyde), before submerging it in the chemical-filled tank.

Fresh liquid may be added to a jar a few weeks after it is made, as bodily fluids such as blood may leak out of the specimen, changing the color of the liquid.

The specimen jar is labeled with the type of species it contains and the date it was stored, as over time the specimen may change, potentially becoming unrecognizable.

The specimens are stored in jars of a suitable size and shape, so that they won't float around and get damaged inside.

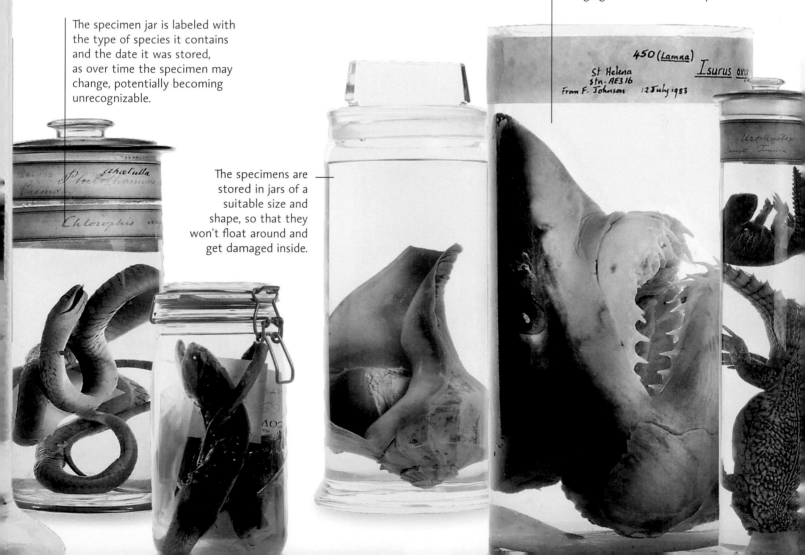

GIANT FISH SPECIMENS

This large ocean sunfish is stored at the Natural History Museum in London, England. Stored in ethanol, the fish has hardly decayed since it was caught in the 1960s. The tank has a heavy metal lid, which has been temporarily removed so that this curator can inspect the fish. In the past, specimen tanks were made from glass but today clear plastic is used, as it costs less, it won't crack or break, and it's lighter if the specimen needs to be moved.

Safety first

London's Natural History Museum has one of the world's biggest fish specimens on display. The tank for this 13-ft (4-m), 772-lb (350-kg) blue marlin takes 2,600 gallons (10,000 liters) of preservative liquid to fill it. Normally conservators would store specimens in ethanol, but it's a flammable chemical, posing a risk to museum visitors. Instead, to make the display tank safe, the blue marlin has been preserved in glycerol—a chemical that isn't flammable or toxic but still preserves well. The fish is suspended by stainless steel cables to weights in the bottom of the tank, so that it doesn't float to the surface.

THE NATURAL HISTORY MUSEUM, ENGLAND

Located at the heart of London, the Natural History Museum welcomes more than 5 million visitors a year. Its 80-million-item collection showcases the history of our planet, from a prehistoric meteorite to dinosaur skeletons, as well as today's plants and animals.

19th-century taxidermists

This photograph, taken around 1880, shows William Temple Hornaday, the chief taxidermist and zoologist of the United States National Museum, working on a mounted animal in the Smithsonian's taxidermy workshop. His work was enjoyed by museum visitors, keen to learn about exotic species they had never seen before.

White penguin feathers darken with time, so they require conservation.

The penguin's eyes were replaced with glass or plastic replicas.

PRESERVED PENGUINS

Taxidermy is the process of preserving a dead animal's body, allowing biologists to study it at a later time, sometimes many years after its death. There are examples of the ancient Egyptians preserving animals in similar ways for religious purposes, but it wasn't until the late 19th century that taxidermy became popular. In the past, mammals, fishes, and birds were filled with straw after their organs and skeletons had been removed, but today taxidermists stretch animal skins, known as hides, over plastic or foam frames.

Maintaining the specimens

Taxidermists clean the display animals regularly to prevent decay and to maintain the hides. Here, a taxidermist is using an airbrush to keep the bear's brown fur in good condition.

▼ Penguin colony

These taxidermied penguins were displayed at the Natural History Museum in Le Havre, northern France, in an exhibit about Antarctica. Each penguin is standing on its own small plinth. They are now in storage.

DID YOU KNOW?

"Taxidermy" comes from the Greek for arrangement (*taxis*) and skin (*derma*).

The soft, fluffy feathers of chicks are known as "down."

Taxidermy mistakes

Although taxidermists try to make their specimens as realistic as possible, such as setting them in lifelike poses, their plans don't always work.

Overstuffed walrus

The conservators working at the Horniman Museum in London, England, in the late 1800s had never seen a walrus before. They filled this specimen with too much stuffing. Today, the walrus is one of the museum's best-loved artifacts.

Misplaced eyes

This long-eared owl at the UCL Grant Museum of Zoology in London has been well preserved, except for the eyes, which have been set at strange angles.

FROZEN
IN TIME

Older taxidermied specimens were often set in neutral poses as these were the easiest to create when stuffing the animals. However, the more modern technique of stretching animal hides over plastic or foam frames helps taxidermists to position the animals in realistic poses. The lion and bears in this collection of taxidermied creatures kept in storage at the Natural History Museum in Vienna, Austria, are poised to strike their prey.

Attention to detail

Here, Paul Rhymer, retired taxidermist at the Smithsonian, sews up the leg of a taxidermied zebra. He uses his knowledge of anatomy to make sure that the shape of the zebra's leg looks exactly like that of a living zebra.

BUTTERFLY DRAWERS

Hundreds of millions of preserved insect specimens are stored in museums worldwide. The Smithsonian's National Museum of Natural History in the US has more than 35 million insect specimens in its collection, 4 million of which are butterflies and moths. The butterfly and moth collection is so large that it can't all be displayed together. The specimens that aren't on display (some of which are shown here) are kept in storage, filling more than 30,000 drawers.

Insect trays

Insect specimens in storage are not hidden away and forgotten about. Instead, they are regularly taken out of their storage boxes to be inspected, cleaned, and studied by biologists. Insects are fragile and normally decompose quickly after death. Preserving them makes it possible to study them for many years after their death. It also allows biologists to research species from around the world, including those that are now extinct.

BONES IN STORAGE

In Maryland, Smithsonian's National Museum of Natural History's whale warehouse contains the world's largest collection of whale bones. Filling the shelves are the bones of more than 10,000 marine mammals, some of which are 40 million years old. But many of the bones were collected during commercial whale-hunting expeditions in the Atlantic Ocean between the late 1700s and mid-1800s. The largest bone in the facility is a 24-ft (7-m) jawbone from a blue whale. It is the largest bone held by any museum in the world. Objects of this size are too heavy to be carried by people, and can only be moved around using fork lifts.

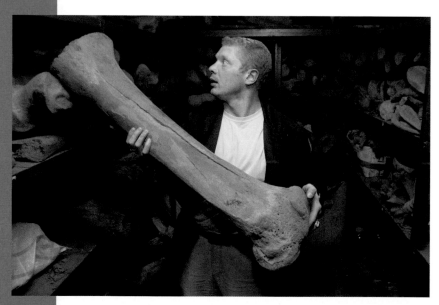

Mammoth bone

Whales aren't the only giant animals found in museum storage rooms. The Ice Age Museum in Moscow, Russia, has huge stores of prehistoric bones from enormous animals that inhabited Earth tens of thousands of years ago. Here, a museum employee holds a giant mammoth thigh bone. Archaeologists in Siberia discovered it after layers of permafrost thawed out due to rising temperatures in the region.

MILITARY STORAGE

Not all museum objects fit into neat storage cupboards and drawers. The Tank Museum in Dorset, England, has 300 huge tanks, from the world's first tank "Little Willie," made in England in 1915, to an example of the "Challenger 2," a British tank still in use today. These tanks all need to be kept somewhere, but the museum has turned this challenge into an asset. Their storage rooms are open to the public, showing how museum storage spaces themselves can become exhibitions. As well as this, they also allow people into their restoration workshops, where visitors can see real tanks being repaired and restored to working order.

Military planes

When a museum's artifacts just won't fit inside, they are sometimes stored outside, like at Pima Air and Space Museum in Arizona. These planes are part of the museum's astonishing display, where hundreds of aircraft are spread out across the desert.

UNUSUAL MUSEUMS

Not every museum is dedicated to priceless artifacts and scientific endeavor. Some of the world's most interesting collections focus on everyday items or strange, unexpected things. Whether the subject is cats or, quite literally, trash, you can guarantee there will be a museum showcasing its variety. A visit to one of these unconventional museums can be fun and highly educational. Be advised, however—some of these quirky institutions are not for the squeamish!

The toilet museum's biggest attraction is this replica of Louis XIV's throne-style toilet.

MUSEUM OF TRASH

This museum in New York was created from more than 1,000 items rescued from people's trash. It records the city's changing neighborhoods through what their inhabitants choose to throw away.

35
The number of years it took to create the museum's collection.

THE SULABH INTERNATIONAL MUSEUM OF TOILETS

This quirky museum in Delhi, India, introduces visitors to the history of toilets. The collection includes a replica of the toilet used by King Louis XIV of France as well as a cushioned armchair toilet. On a more serious note, the museum draws attention to the deaths of about half a million children every year in India related to unhygienic toilet facilities and poor plumbing.

CHOCOLATE MUSEUM

This museum in Cologne, Germany, reveals the history of chocolate from its origins in Central America in around 450 BCE to the way it is made in factories today. Visitors can discover for themselves how chocolate is made by roasting and grinding cocoa beans in the museum's in-house production facility, and see the enormous chocolate fountain, which was specially constructed for the museum.

MUSEUM OF TAP WATER

Beijing's Museum of Tap Water is located in an apartment complex on the site of China's first water treatment plant. The unusual museum showcases the history of the city's clean water pipelines.

THE MEGURO PARASITOLOGICAL MUSEUM

This museum in Japan's capital city, Tokyo, houses thousands of parasite specimens and details their impact on human and animal hosts. The highlight is a 30-ft (9-m) tapeworm, which had been removed from a man three months after he had eaten raw fish.

45,000

The number of specimens in the museum.

CAT MUSEUM

Five thousand years of feline history are exhibited at the Cat Museum in Kuching, Malaysia, which includes a mummified cat from ancient Egypt.

4,000

The number of artifacts in the museum.

BEST OF THE REST

▶ **MUSEUM OF BAD ART**
As the name suggests, this privately owned museum in Massachusetts is dedicated to exhibiting the best examples of bad art.

▶ **EUROPEAN BREAD MUSEUM**
The 6,000-year history of bread is displayed through 18,000 artifacts and artworks in this museum in Germany.

▶ **THE PARIS SEWER MUSEUM**
Five hundred years of waste-disposal history is showcased in this underground museum in Paris, France.

▶ **CANCUN UNDERWATER MUSEUM**
Coral reefs near Cancun, Mexico, were being damaged by tourists, boats, and divers, so this underwater sculpture park was built to stop people swimming near the vulnerable reefs.

Museums work hard to preserve the past so that future generations can learn about and understand history. Whether figuring out the safest way to raise a Tudor shipwreck from the ocean floor or restoring antique armor to its former glory, highly skilled conservators protect amazing artifacts from decay, deterioration, and pesky pests. Without the expertise of conservators, many historical items would end up damaged beyond repair or even be lost forever.

SAVING HISTORY

4

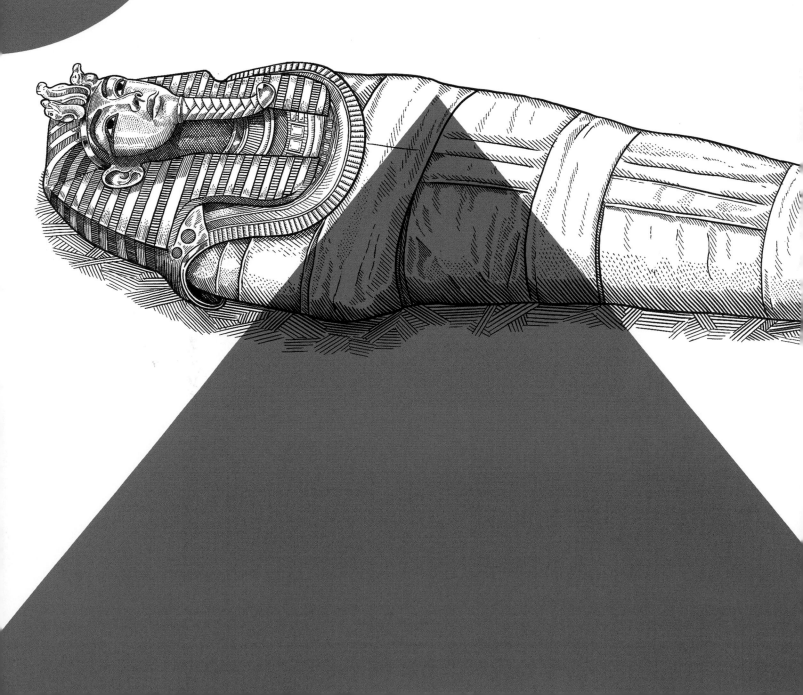

CONSERVATOR

A conservator is responsible for making sure that historical artifacts stay in good condition, so that they can be seen and studied by future generations of people. Conservators control the conditions an artifact is kept in, regulating the light, temperature, and humidity to which it's exposed. In some cases, they might also have to fix broken artifacts, making sure that the repairs they make are as invisible as possible. Most conservators have a speciality—from books and pottery to ancient statues and dinosaur fossils.

Repair and restore
If an artifact has been accidentally broken, a conservator repairs it, ensuring that the object looks exactly as it did originally. At the Palace Museum in China, these conservators are fixing a delicate porcelain bowl.

Careful cleaning

Conservators spend a lot of time cleaning delicate artifacts that have become dirty over time. They try not to cause any damage to the artifacts, so often they simply use tiny brushes to gently remove dirt. Some artifacts may need to be treated with cleaning chemicals, however. In these situations, a conservator will carry out tests before starting to clean the artifact to find out what materials it is made from, and how these materials will react with different types of chemicals.

FIRST SUIT ON THE MOON

In 1969, American astronaut Neil Armstrong became the first person to walk on the Moon. His custom-built spacesuit protected him from the extreme temperatures and shielded him from radiation from the sun. The suit was designed to last for just a few months and today, 50 years after the historic Moon landing, the materials it's made from are fast disintegrating (breaking down). Keeping the suit in the same condition as it was when Armstrong returned from the Apollo 11 mission is a huge challenge for conservators.

The suit's structure includes 21 layers of material.

Apollo 11 spacesuits

The suits worn by the astronauts on the Apollo 11 mission—Neil Armstrong, Edwin "Buzz" Aldrin, Jr., and Michael Collins—were built to withstand the wide range of temperatures on the Moon, radiation from the sun, and fast-traveling particles. The suits weighed about 80 lb (36 kg) each. On Earth, they would have felt heavy, but in the low-gravity environment of the Moon, they felt much lighter.

▶ Self-destructing materials

Armstrong's spacesuit is made from synthetic materials that produce acidic gases in a process known as "off-gassing." The gases released cause damage. In some places on the suit, two or more different materials are in contact with one another, which accelerates the speed of disintegration. For example, the zipper is made from rubber and copper—two substances that react negatively with each other, causing them to break down.

Moon dust

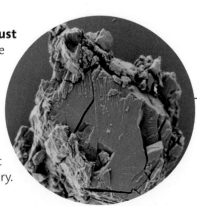

After the Apollo 11 mission, the gloves and lower parts of the suit were covered in Moon dust. Grains of Moon dust are very sharp, as this photograph taken with a scanning electron microscope shows. Conservators have left the dust in place, as it is an important part of the suit's history.

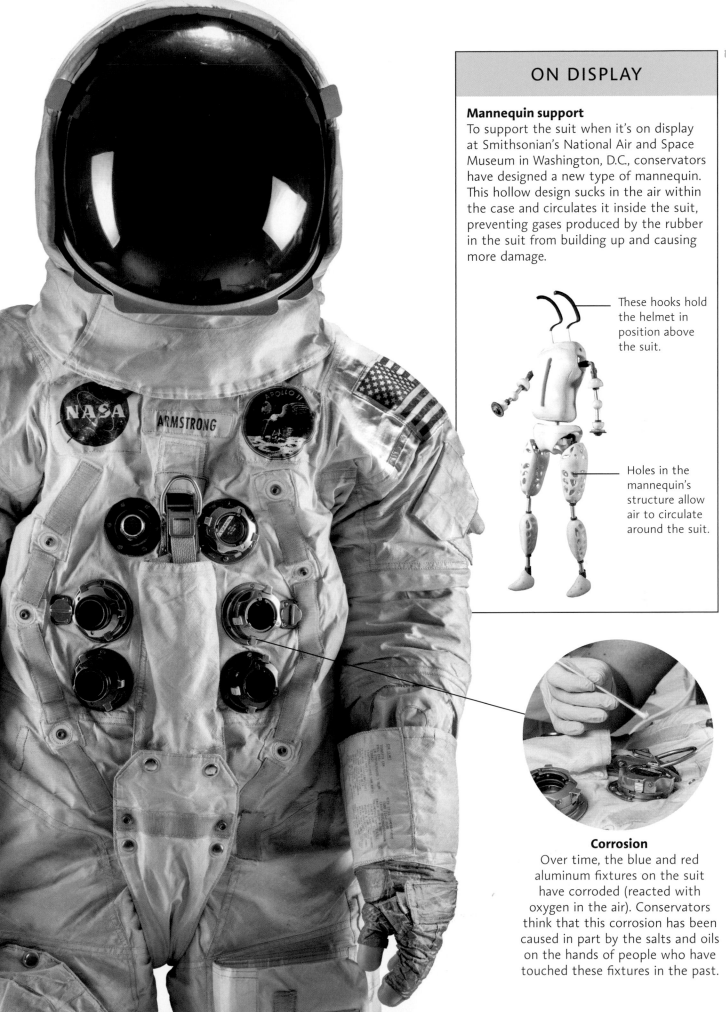

ON DISPLAY

Mannequin support

To support the suit when it's on display at Smithsonian's National Air and Space Museum in Washington, D.C, conservators have designed a new type of mannequin. This hollow design sucks in the air within the case and circulates it inside the suit, preventing gases produced by the rubber in the suit from building up and causing more damage.

These hooks hold the helmet in position above the suit.

Holes in the mannequin's structure allow air to circulate around the suit.

Corrosion

Over time, the blue and red aluminum fixtures on the suit have corroded (reacted with oxygen in the air). Conservators think that this corrosion has been caused in part by the salts and oils on the hands of people who have touched these fixtures in the past.

SPACESUITS IN STORAGE

The world's largest collection of spacesuits from the US Space Program are kept in a storage facility at the Steven F. Udvar-Hazy Center, part of the National Air and Space Museum in Virginia. A team of conservators works to preserve and conserve these historic suits. There are more than 200 suits in storage and, just like Neil Armstrong's suit, many are deteriorating. To help prevent further damage, the suits are kept in humidity-controlled conditions and stored at around 60°F (16°C).

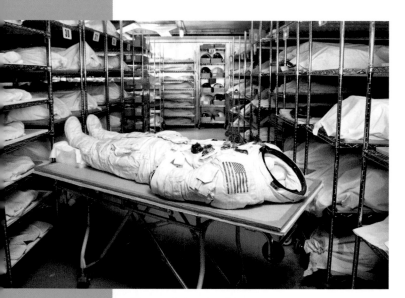

In cold conditions

All the helmets and gloves are stored separately from the spacesuits. Leaving the helmets and gloves off the suits allows fresh air to circulate inside them, preventing the buildup of any gases produced by the suits as they deteriorate. Specialists regularly monitor light levels in the room, too, as exposure to light can cause permanent damage that can't be repaired.

RAISING THE MARY ROSE

Henry VIII was the King of England between 1509 and 1547. Launched in 1511, the *Mary Rose* was one of the flagships of his fleet. It sank defending England from an invading French fleet during the Battle of the Solent in July 1545. Apart from a brief investigation by pioneering divers in the 1830s, the *Mary Rose* lay on the seabed for 426 years before the hull was rediscovered in 1971. The ship was then raised from the seabed and preserved for future generations.

◀ Sunken ship

The 115-ft (35-m) ship was raised from the seabed in 1982 using a specially designed lifting frame and cradle. The hull (the main body of the ship) was attached to the frame by steel bolts and cables, and then carefully moved onto the cradle that had been placed next to it on the seabed. It was then raised gently above the water by a crane.

Soaking artifacts

When archaeologists raised the *Mary Rose*, they also brought to the surface a huge number of artifacts, including this enormous anchor. Many of the artifacts were kept in water tanks while the museum team decided how best to conserve them.

Underwater discoveries

Around 19,000 artifacts were discovered within the hull of the *Mary Rose*, giving us an insight into the everyday life of the crew. Archaeologists even found the skeleton of the ship's dog.

The museum team nicknamed the ship's dog "Hatch."

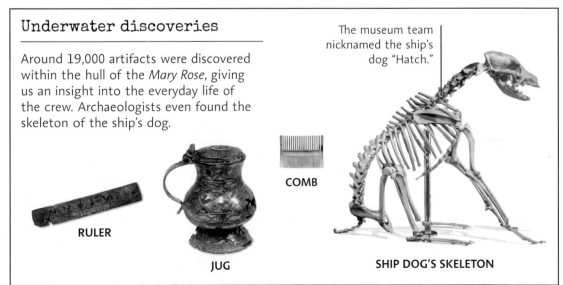

RULER

JUG

COMB

SHIP DOG'S SKELETON

TUDOR TREASURE

When the *Mary Rose* was brought to the surface in 1982, it was very fragile. It took conservators years to stabilize the ship's condition. Its wooden timbers had to be kept wet as they would warp and crack if they dried out too quickly, so the ship was sprayed continuously—first with water and then with polyethylene glycol (PEG), a chemical that replaced the water inside the soaked timbers, helping the ship hold its structure. In 2013, more than 30 years after the ship was raised, conservators decided it was stable enough to be dried out and they stopped spraying it with PEG. The *Mary Rose* is on permanent display in the carefully monitored temperature- and humidity-controlled Weston Ship Hall in Portsmouth, England.

THE MARY ROSE MUSEUM, ENGLAND

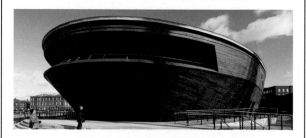

The purpose-built Mary Rose Museum in Portsmouth opened in 2013. It was built in and around a dry dock (a large basin) in which the hull of the *Mary Rose* was displayed. Conservation work on the ship continued throughout construction.

CANNON RESTORATION

Even battle-scarred weaponry can be restored to its former glory. At Les Invalides, a center for military history in Paris, France, a talented team took on the task of restoring this 18th-century Prussian cannon. Their careful and successful use of some seemingly brutal techniques shows that not all museum restorations are delicate processes.

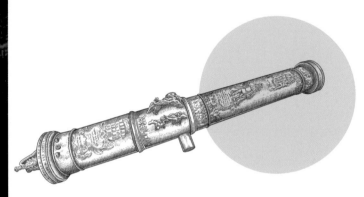

Delicate detail

This bronze cannon is particularly ornate for a weapon of war. It features many intricate designs, including this depiction of a high-ranking Prussian official.

◄ Sandblasting

1 Technicians started by sandblasting the cannon to clean it. A high-pressure stream of sand rubbed away dirt and rust from the cannon.

Removing moisture

2 Next, a trio of gas-powered torches were used to heat up the cannon, causing any moisture from the metal to evaporate.

Waxing and protecting

3 While the cannon was still warm from the torch treatment, a layer of wax was applied to protect the bronze and make it shine, completing the restoration.

SUFFRAGETTE SCRAPBOOK

Lots of important historical artifacts are made from paper, which is a long-lasting material if cared for properly. Ada Flatman was a British suffragette who made scrapbooks containing newspaper clippings, flyers, and photographs of the suffragettes' struggle to win the vote for women in the early 20th century. These scrapbooks are tricky to preserve as they contain different types of paper.

Paper conservation ▶

The materials in Flatman's scrapbooks have lasted a long time, although they have weakened with age. There are tiny tears in the paper and some paper fragments have come unstuck. To preserve their condition, the conservator carefully cleaned each page with a chemical sponge, and repaired tears in the paper with glue and tengujo, a very thin and fibrous material that reinforces the original paper.

Preserving memories
This is one of three scrapbooks Ada Flatman created between 1908 and 1912. It is kept at the Museum of London in England.

In some places, the paper had been folded or creased, making it especially brittle.

A magnifying glass allows the conservator to examine the scrapbook's condition in detail.

DEEDS NOT WORDS

DID YOU · KNOW?

In 1893, New Zealand became the first country in the world to give women the right to vote.

The conservator uses brushes of varying sizes, from wide to narrow, to carry out the repairs.

Antarctic notebook

In 2012, New Zealand's Antarctic Heritage Trust discovered a 102-year-old notebook in the Antarctic from Captain Scott's voyage to the South Pole. Ravaged by exposure to the harsh environment, it needed to be delicately restored.

1 The notebook's original binding had disintegrated, so the conservator started the restoration by separating the pages and laying out the pieces needing repair.

2 The conservator then painstakingly reconstructed each page using tengujo before scanning them to create a digital copy of the notebook.

3 Finally, the conservator sewed the pages back together and used the original cover to bind the notebook.

GREEDY GRUBS

Textiles, wooden objects, and animal specimens are just some of the tasty treats found in museums that pesky pests will feast on. Museums must keep a very close eye on how they display and store their items, as a bad pest infestation could easily damage or destroy precious artifacts.

▼ Munching paper

Silverfish are destructive bugs that love to feast on paper. They thrive in dark, damp environments, so museum staff must make sure that humidity levels are kept in check to stop these bugs from destroying paper artifacts.

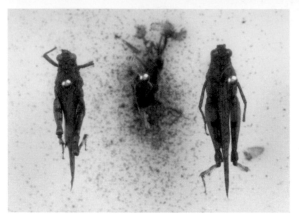

Insect-eating insects

Insects will feast on just about anything in a museum … even other insects! Here, one of the London Natural History Museum's grasshopper specimens has been eaten by a common carpet beetle (*Anthrenus scrophulariae*).

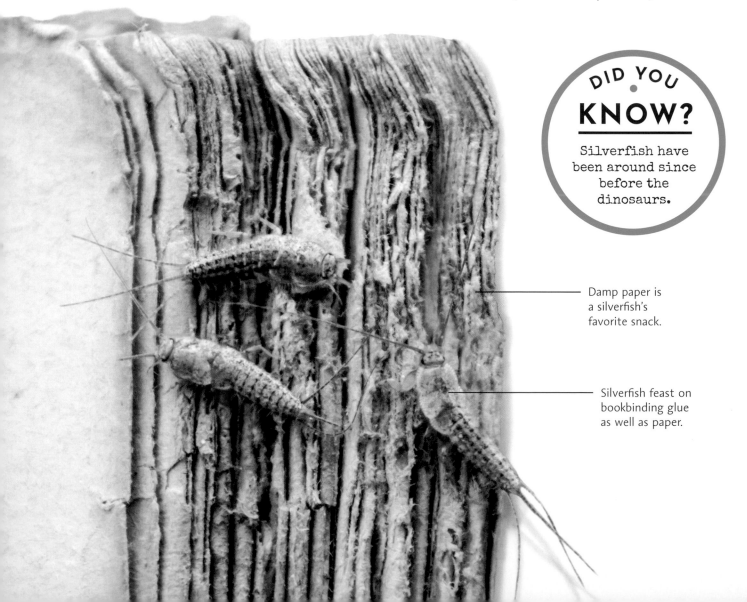

DID YOU KNOW?

Silverfish have been around since before the dinosaurs.

Damp paper is a silverfish's favorite snack.

Silverfish feast on bookbinding glue as well as paper.

Riley's harness shows that he is a member of the MFA's Protective Services and Conservation Team.

Controlling pests

In the past, museums often used toxic chemicals to kill pests, but this can harm humans and the collections, so some now use "anoxic treatments." Here, museum workers are creating an airtight chamber around some infested items. Inside, they place packets of iron filings, which draw oxygen out of the air as they rust. What's left is an oxygen-free atmosphere, which kills off the pests.

Pest–control puppy

In 2018, Boston's Museum of Fine Arts (MFA) took on a new pest controller named Riley. With his unmatched sense of smell, this Weimaraner puppy is trained to detect the scent of harmful insects and alert museum staff by barking.

Types of pest

Many museums will have a pest management plan in place to deal with infestations. These plans must protect against invasive animals such as rodents, birds, and bats, as well as insects whose small size often allows them to creep in undetected, causing permanent damage.

Webbing clothes moth
These pests nest and feed on natural fibers and skins. Conservators sometimes use glue boards infused with a female mating hormone to lure male moths onto the sticky surface, trapping them.

Woodworm
Woodworms eat their way through wooden objects, causing enormous damage. Conservators can control an infestation by placing the contaminated item in a freezer for three days at -22°F (-30°C), which kills all the larvae.

Woolly bear
Carpet beetle larvae are commonly known as "woolly bears," perhaps because of their hairy appearance. These furry bugs love to eat wool, fur, and feathers, so textiles and animal specimens need to be regularly vacuumed and inspected.

Fixing the stitching
A linen lining was attached to the back of the flag many years ago as part of early conservation work. Unfortunately, this was doing more harm than good, so the conservators removed it, snipping away 1.7 million stitches.

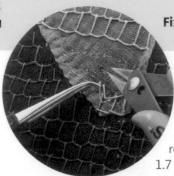

Cleaning with sponges
The conservators used dry sponges to remove dirt from the surface of the flag. They then applied a solution of cleaning chemicals and water to remove dangerous pollutants.

STAR-SPANGLED BANNER

The United States flag was first used in 1777. But it was a particular flag made in 1813 that became known as the Star-Spangled Banner. The 30 ft by 42 ft (9 m by 12 m) flag symbolized lasting independence and inspired the national anthem of the same name. The flag was so popular that pieces of it were cut away as souvenirs. Consequently it has lost 8 ft (2.4 m) of its length and has holes where pieces were taken.

◀ The Star-Spangled Banner

General George Armistead requested a new flag to fly over Fort McHenry in Baltimore as a display of American strength and defiance. It was sewn by Mary Pickersgill with the design of the time, which featured 15 stars and 15 stripes to represent each of the US states. The project to conserve the Star-Spangled Banner cost $7 million (£5.5 million).

Knotty fibers
To check the condition of the flag, conservators removed tiny samples of the material and looked at them at 3,000x magnification. This let them see microscopic damage, so that they could act to prevent further deterioration.

Threadbare textiles
A lot of the flag's material has disintegrated with time, leaving it very fragile. Conservators stabilized the flag by sewing it onto a type of polyester called Stabilex, and adding a new underlay.

ON DISPLAY

The correct angle
The flag is on display at the National Museum of American History. It used to hang from the wall, but it now lies in a climate- and light-controlled room, displayed at an angle that doesn't put too much strain on the material.

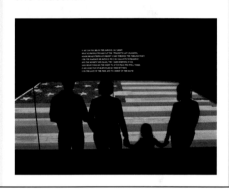

NATIONAL MUSEUM OF AMERICAN HISTORY, US

Founded in 1964 in Washington, D.C., this museum is part of the Smithsonian Institution. It houses the world's largest collection dedicated to US history. The museum has more than 1.8 million items on display and welcomes around 4 million visitors per year.

THE OSEBERG SHIP

The Vikings were Scandinavian seafarers who lived between the 8th and 11th centuries. They were excellent ship builders and traveled huge distances by sea, as far as North America to the West and the Caspian Sea in the East. Built in around 820, the Oseberg Ship was found in 1903 on a farm in Norway. Almost complete, it had been placed in a pit in around 834 and covered with soil to form a burial mound for two Viking women. After archaeologists finished excavating the ship in 1904, conservators spent the next 21 years drying, restoring, and reassembling it.

▶ Viking treasures

Inside the ship, archaeologists found the bodies of two women who had been buried inside it—one in her 80s and the other in her 50s. They also found a cart; four sleighs; the bodies of a number of horses, cattle, and dogs; expensive fabrics; ornaments; and household goods, as well as five carved animal-head posts inside the ship.

The deck of the ship was made from planks of pinewood.

The pine mast was over 33 ft (10 m) high. The ship could be sailed as well as rowed.

The hull was built with oak planks, which were secured with iron rivets.

The 15 oar holes on each side of the ship suggest that it took 30 people to power the boat.

THE VIKING SHIP MUSEUM, NORWAY

This Viking Ship Museum is part of the Museum of Cultural History in Oslo, Norway. It showcases three brilliantly preserved Viking longships, and attracts 600,000 visitors every year. It also houses all of the artifacts found with the ships.

Tiny details
Intended for a wealthy or high-status person, the Oseberg Ship was beautifully decorated, with many intricate carvings.

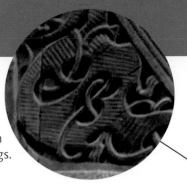

The prow (the front part of the ship above the waterline) was curved into a spiraling serpent's head.

A ship unearthed

Once discovered underneath the mound of earth, the ship was excavated by a team of archaeologists in less than three months. The damp soil had kept the vessel almost completely intact so it was in excellent condition.

Wood treatment

In the early 1900s, conservators treated the wooden ship, and the artifacts buried with it, with alum to dry them out. Unfortunately, this treatment weakened the wooden artifacts, a problem that conservators are still working out how to fix today.

▶ Conservation challenge

The conservators found that dirt, pests, and changing temperatures had damaged some of the armor. The armor had been created from a wide variety of materials, including leather, horn, metal, textile, and urushi (a type of lacquer). Each of these materials required different methods and cleaning liquids to stabilize them before the armor could be put on display.

SAMURAI ARMOR BEFORE TREATMENT

There is intricate decoration on the armor.

Adding netting
Conservators strengthened some of the damaged and fragile textile using nylon netting, secured in place with silk thread.

Removing pests
More than 100 insect skins found underneath the silk on the breastplate were carefully removed using tweezers.

This stencilled leather would originally have been brightly colored but has faded over time due to exposure to light.

Conservators used glue to mend the urushi lacquer on the suit. Urushi is made from tree resin.

Textile parts, like this tassel, are particularly delicate.

SAMURAI ARMOR

In 2018, the British Museum in London, England, acquired a set of 18th-century Japanese armor. It would have once been worn by a samurai, a member of a powerful warrior class that existed in Japan from the 12th to the 19th century. The armor, an example of samurai ceremonial dress rather than actual battle armor, needed more than 250 hours of conservation work before it could be exhibited. The items had previously been owned by a private collector, so there were no condition records, making the task all the more challenging.

Cleaning the armor

When the armor first arrived at the museum, it was put into quarantine, away from all the other artifacts in the museum, for several months in case it contained pests that could infest and damage other artifacts. The conservator then cleaned it with a soft brush and a small vacuum to suck up the dust.

ON DISPLAY

Wooden stand

After more than 250 hours of work carried out over eight months, the armor was ready to display. It is supported in its display case by a wooden stand, parts of which are padded to protect the armor from being scratched and to add shape to it.

SMALL MUSEUMS

Museum collections are often housed in big buildings with grand display halls, but for small objects or exhibitions, small spaces can do the job just as well. Old elevators and even disused telephone booths can be transformed to showcase fascinating artifacts, although only one person may be able to see them at a time! Some small museums are themselves dedicated to tiny artifacts and specimens barely visible to the naked eye. From microscopic life forms to miniscule artworks, not all objects have to be big to grab your attention.

HOOSESAGG MUSEUM

People passing by in Basel, Switzerland, can peer in at this tiny museum, housed behind a 600-year-old window. The display changes every month and contains a collection of memorabilia, including small perfume bottles, bells, watches, and snow globes. As most of the items on display are small enough to fit in your pocket, the owners named it the Hoosesagg (Pants Pocket) Museum.

Photographs of important past residents as well as local artifacts fit inside this old phone booth.

WARLEY MUSEUM

The residents of Warley Town, a small village in England, didn't want an old, disused telephone booth to go to waste, so they turned it into a museum to reflect the history of their village.

Large-scale models of microbes let visitors see what these organisms look like.

MICROPIA

A visit to Micropia in Amsterdam, Netherlands, reveals the hidden world of the tiny life forms we call microbes—from bacteria and viruses to water fleas and eyelash mites. The museum teaches visitors that although some of these microbes can make us ill, without others, life on earth would not be possible.

MICRARIUM

In London, England, the UCL Grant Museum of Zoology turned a tiny space in the museum into a Micrarium—a "place for small things." Inside is a vast collection of microscope slides revealing the diversity of animal life.

2,323

The number of microscope slides displayed in the Micrarium.

MYKOLA SYADRISTY MICROMINIATURES MUSEUM

This museum in Kiev, Ukraine, is dedicated to micro art—miniature drawings, sculptures, and other works of art all hand-made by a self-taught artist, Mykola Syadristy. Visitors have to view them through magnifying glasses to see all of their miniscule detail.

A sculpture of a pyramid and a camel train sits within the eye of this needle.

MMUSEUMM

This old freight elevator in New York showcases everyday objects such as toothpaste and an umbrella. They aren't just ordinary objects, though—they all have a story to tell. Even when the museum is closed, visitors can see the artifacts through peepholes in the doors. The quirky collection changes every year.

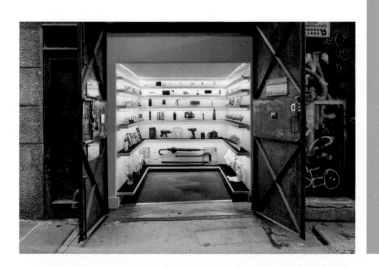

BEST OF THE REST

▶ MIMUMO

This tiny museum, just 25 sq ft (2.3 sq m) in size, is housed in one of the oldest houses in Monza, Italy. It showcases the works of various artists and is open every day of the year, 24 hours a day.

▶ EDGAR'S CLOSET

A school room in Alabama houses hundreds of objects relating to the American writer Edgar Allan Poe.

▶ TINY E'S MUSEUM

This museum dedicated to Elvis Presley is based in a trailer which travels around the US.

COLLECTIONS
CLEANING

Cleaning valuable, and often fragile, artifacts is a specialized task carried out by conservators. Museum items must be cleaned thoroughly, but also carefully. The main aim of keeping artifacts clean isn't so that they look good on display, it's to protect and preserve them. If not kept in check, dust, grime, and insects (attracted by the dirt) can build up and cause irreversible damage.

▼ Saliva-cleaning

After years of people touching the Royal Alberta Museum's "finger rock" in Canada, a layer of grease and dirt collected on its surface. Conservators decided to use saliva as a cleaning agent as it contains amylase, a substance that effectively breaks down dirt. Conservator Susan Green "spit-cleaned" the rock using her own saliva on cotton swabs.

Hidey-holes
When cleaning out the many holes on the rock's surface, the conservator found bits of pencils, a stick, and several coins.

String was used to divide the rock into sections so the conservator could work methodically.

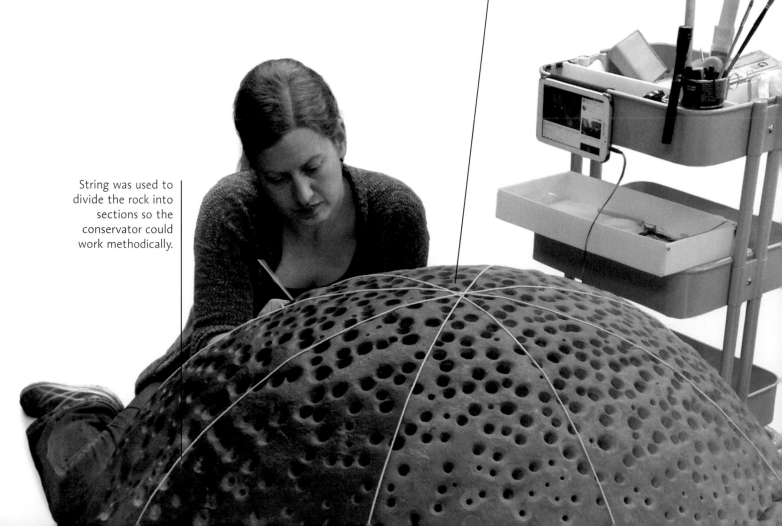

Conservator's toolkit

A specialized task requires specialized tools. Here are some of the things conservators use to keep museum artifacts free from harmful substances.

Soft brushes are used to remove surface debris.

Disposable pipettes are used for applying liquids in a controlled way.

Chemicals are used sparingly, but they can be very effective.

Large stencil brushes can be used with care on more robust surfaces.

Syringes are used to access hard-to-reach places.

Gloves protect artifacts from oils and grease found on the hands of people who touch them.

Very sharp medical scalpels are used to carefully cut away dirt or defects without damaging the underlying surface.

Different-sized sponges, both natural and synthetic, are used to remove dirt.

Mesh frames are placed over fragile textiles while they are vacuumed. They prevent the suction of the vacuum from ripping the fragile material underneath.

Cleaning techniques

Museum conservators are responsible for all sorts of objects, made from many different materials including stone, paper, wood, or metal. They use various cleaning techniques depending on the type of object they're working on.

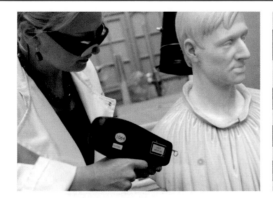

Laser cleaning
Old stone or marble statues can be cleaned using lasers, which destroy dirt without damaging the statues themselves. Scientists are still researching the best types of laser to use for this process.

Sucking up dust
Rather than directly applying a vacuum cleaner to an artifact, which may damage it, conservators often use a soft brush to dislodge dust, and vacuum up that dust from a slight distance away.

The top of the mask is decorated with a cobra—a symbol that represented lower Egypt. The vulture next to it represents higher Egypt.

◀ **The Pharaoh's burial mask**

While fixing Tutankhamen's beard, the experts carried out the first thorough survey of the burial mask. It is 2 ft (54 cm) tall and made from more than 20 lb (9 kg) of gold. It is decorated with pieces of glass and jewels, and there is text from the ancient Egyptian "Book of the Dead" inscribed on the back of the mask in hieroglyphics.

The dark blue stripes across the mask are made from glass.

FIXING A PHARAOH

In 1922, a team of archaeologists, including Englishman Howard Carter, found the tomb of Tutankhamen, a young pharaoh (ruler), in the Valley of the Kings in Egypt. It had not been opened for 3,300 years. Inside, among other treasures, Carter's team found Tutankhamen's burial mask, which had been placed over the head of the pharaoh's preserved body. In 2014, at the Egyptian Museum in Cairo, Egypt, the mask's beard was accidentally snapped off, damaging the priceless artifact.

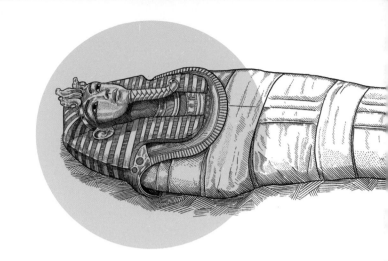

Tutankhamen's tomb

Tutankhamen was buried with more than 5,000 items, believed to help him in the afterlife, including a golden throne. When archaeologists discovered the tomb, they were shocked to find all of these items still inside. Most of the other tombs in the Valley of the Kings had been targeted by thieves who had taken any items of value.

Damage repair

When the beard was broken off, the museum workers reattached it using a glue known as epoxy resin. This strong substance leaked out of the join between the chin and beard so they tried to remove it, damaging the mask. To fix the botched repair, a team of Egyptian and German experts heated the mask to soften the excess glue. They then used wooden rods to scrape it away, before reattaching the beard with beeswax, a traditional ancient Egyptian glue.

Here, the conservator uses a wooden rod to remove the epoxy resin.

STATUE REPAIR

During wars, fighting and violence often leads to destruction, including damage to cultural objects, meaning that artifacts that might give us invaluable insights into the lives of people in the past are lost. In 2015, during the Syrian civil war, the UNESCO World Heritage Site of Palmyra was attacked and many of the city's ancient treasures were stolen and destroyed. In the aftermath of the attack, conservators were determined to restore as much of the site to its former glory as possible.

▲ Identifying damage

This statue, a funerary bust dating back to the 2nd century CE, was badly damaged during attacks on Palmyra. In 2017, experts were able to put part of it back together, but half of the face was completely missing.

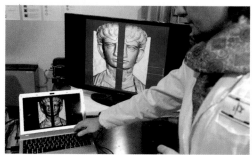

◀ Mirror image

Scientists in Rome, Italy, used lasers to scan the statue's face. They used a mirror image of the undamaged half to digitally recreate what the broken half would have looked like.

◀ Designing the missing piece

Using these scans and mirror images, the team meticulously designed a prosthetic (an artificial body part) to replace the missing piece of the statue.

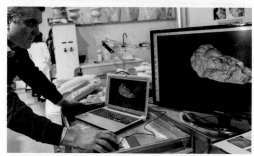

◀ Creating the missing piece

The scientists then used a 3-D printer to produce the replacement piece. It was printed in resin, which forms a hard plastic.

DID YOU KNOW?

Thousands of artifacts were moved to safety before attacks began.

▶ Attached by magnets
The team attached the prosthetic to the bust using six magnets, so it can be safely removed if the missing stone fragments are ever found.

MAGNETS ON THE PROSTHETIC

MAGNETS ON THE STATUE

▶ Restored treasure
With the prosthetic in place, the bust is restored. Its damage is now part of its story. The statue has since been returned to Palmyra.

The prosthetic fits perfectly into the damaged section.

The bust has inscriptions in two languages, Ancient Greek and Aramaic.

The clothing indicates that the man may have been a member of the elite merchant class.

The attackers used hammers to cause this damage to the statue.

ROSA PARKS'S
PROTEST

On December 1, 1955, Rosa Parks, an African American passenger aboard bus number 2857 in Montgomery, Alabama, was asked to give up her seat to a white man. She refused, breaking the racist laws that aimed to separate black people and white people at the time. This act of courage made Parks a lasting symbol of the civil rights movement in the US.

Complex project

In 2001, The Henry Ford Museum bought the bus on which Rosa Parks was traveling for $492,000 (£375,000). The bus needed a lot of work to restore it to its original condition. The project cost over $500,000 (£380,000). The restoration was carried out by members of the International Association of Machinists and Aerospace Workers.

Out in the field
Despite its significance to the civil rights movement, bus number 2857 stood unused and rusting in a field in Alabama for 30 years. The windows were broken and the engine and seats had been removed.

Being fixed
The team restored the windows, interior, paint job, and fittings to what they would have looked like in 1955. Engineers even rebuilt the missing engine using parts from similar vehicles.

◄ Bus restoration

The bus was restored to the condition it was in when Rosa Parks made her protest in 1955. Today, it is on display at the Henry Ford Museum of American Innovation, where it remains one of their most popular artifacts.

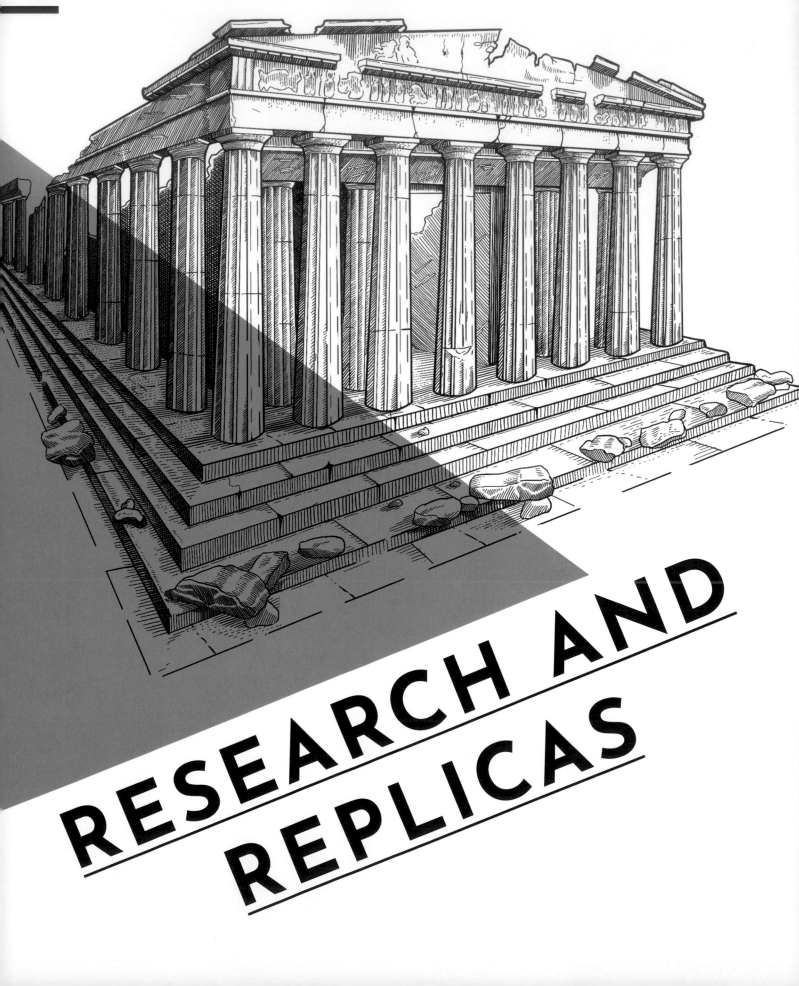

RESEARCH AND REPLICAS

Museums are more than just exhibition spaces. Behind the scenes, researchers study artifacts to uncover as much as possible about the past. Their work can be incredibly varied—it might involve restoring an ancient Greek statue's original coloring, using just a skull to accurately imagine what some of our ancient ancestors' faces may have looked like, or using natural history specimens to help us understand and protect the environment. They also use their expertise to create astonishingly accurate replicas, so crowds of curious visitors can see historical items without harming the precious, fragile originals.

MAKING FACES

When archaeologists find a human skull, they can collaborate with other scientists and sculptors to create a lifelike model of what that person might have looked like. This "facial reconstruction" is a mix of anatomy, art, and history, and it helps us imagine our ancient ancestors who lived and died thousands of years ago.

Facing the past

Swedish facial reconstruction specialist Oscar Nilsson, and a team of scientists working with him, created this model of a teenage girl who lived almost 9,000 years ago. In 1993, her skull was found in the Theopetra Cave (in what is now central Greece). They named her Avgi, the Greek word for "dawn."

THE ACROPOLIS MUSEUM, GREECE

Housing ancient Greek objects, the Acropolis Museum in Athens, Greece, was built to replace an older museum that could no longer hold the enormous number of artifacts being discovered nearby. The museum opened in 2009 and has welcomed 14.5 million visitors in its first 10 years. It holds more than 4,000 objects.

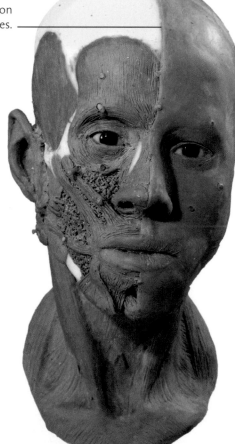

Layers of clay put "flesh" on Avgi's bones.

The 3-D replica is missing teeth, just like Avgi's skull.

Given her likely ethnicity, Avgi probably had dark eyes.

1 Replica skull
Using images taken with a Computed Tomography (CT) scanner—a machine that takes pictures of an object from different angles—the team produced a 3-D–printed replica of Avgi's skull to use as the base for the sculpture.

2 Clay muscles
The team then inserted small plastic pegs into the replica skull. These pegs show how deep the layers of clay, which represent Avgi's facial muscles, should be.

3 Fleshing out
Layer by layer, more details are added to the model. Researchers estimated how much flesh to add to the replica skull, based on factors such as Avgi's age, build, and ethnicity.

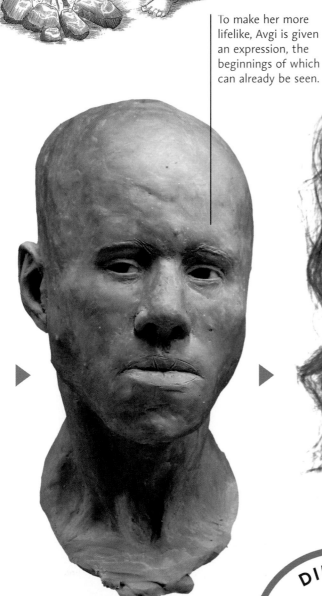

To make her more lifelike, Avgi is given an expression, the beginnings of which can already be seen.

Almost formed

A face starts to emerge in the sculpted model, making it possible to see how Avgi would have looked thousands of years ago.

DID YOU KNOW?

A model such as this can take about 220 hours to complete.

Finished face

A final silicone "skin" is shaped over the face. Hair, eyelashes, and eyebrows are then added, bringing Avgi to life. The model is now on display at the Acropolis Museum in Athens, Greece.

TRUE COLORS

Most of the marble statues from the ancient world still surviving today appear cream or white. But this wasn't always the case. A closer look tells experts that most of them were once decorated with brightly colored paints. This statue from the island of Chios, Greece, was created in around 520 BCE. Centuries of exposure to weather and sunlight have caused its colors to fade, but some traces of the original paint can still be detected.

▶ Color research

Scientists used a variety of techniques to reveal the statue's original colors. They used ultraviolet and infrared light to help them see the traces of paint invisible to the naked eye. They then took samples of these traces and carried out chemical tests on them.

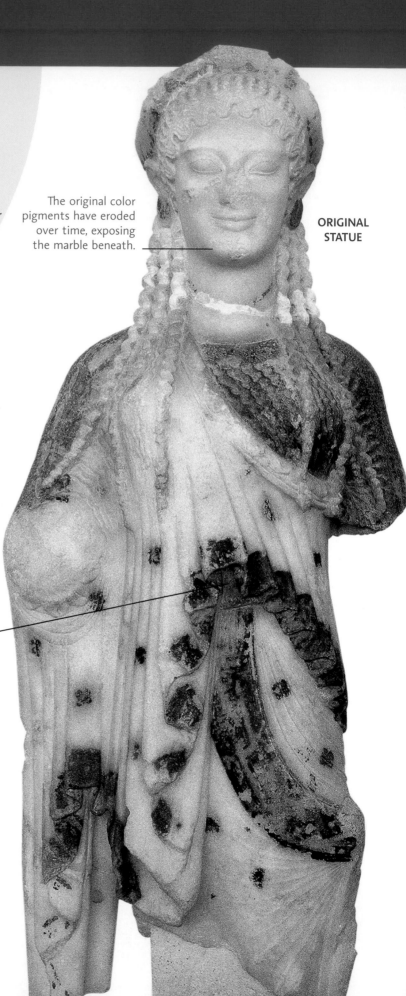

The original color pigments have eroded over time, exposing the marble beneath.

ORIGINAL STATUE

Natural pigments
The ancient Greeks used pigments (dyes) mixed with egg or beeswax to make paint. Some paint colors were poisonous, however: red was made from the chemical mercury and yellow from arsenic.

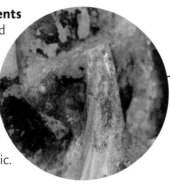

This is a replica (an exact copy) of the original statue. It has been decorated with the colors and patterns that researchers proved were once visible on the original statue.

REPLICA STATUE

The replica's arm has been left unfixed.

Original state

This statue of Paris, an ancient Greek prince, was once on display outside the Temple of Aphaia on the Greek island of Aigina. Over time, the statue had been damaged, so experts made a version to look like it would have originally.

1 Originally, the statue would have been holding a bow and arrow, but these are missing. The statue's nose and ankle have also been destroyed.

2 Experts made a mold of the original statue and then filled it with plaster to make a replica. The nose, ankle, and bow and arrow missing from the original statue were recreated for the replica.

The statue holds a spare arrow.

3 The statue of Paris was then painted as it would have appeared in ancient times. Images of mythical beasts and lions cover his tunic.

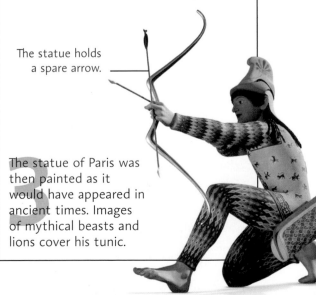

THE SUTTON HOO HELMET

When Edith Pretty asked archaeologist Basil Brown to investigate a mound of earth on her property in Sutton Hoo, England, in 1939, neither of them was expecting it to reveal one of the most important historical discoveries in English history. Hidden under the ground were the remains of a 7th-century Anglo-Saxon ship burial. Full of fabulous treasures, this grave was for an important warrior, or perhaps even a king. Pretty donated everything she found to the British Museum.

Other Sutton Hoo finds

Although the helmet often steals the limelight, an entire treasure trove of jewelry, silverware, and everyday objects was found at the burial site.

Belt buckle
This iron and gold belt buckle is decorated with writhing snakes and other beasts. Its owner would have been a wealthy individual.

Sword handle
War equipment was also discovered at the site, including this sword handle. Experts think that its owner was probably left-handed.

▶ The Sutton Hoo helmet

The most prized artifact found onboard the burial ship was a warrior's helmet made of metal, including iron and copper. Originally discovered as hundreds of fragments, the helmet was painstakingly put together. The first restoration attempt was completed by 1947, but later research raised concerns over the accuracy, prompting another attempt in 1968.

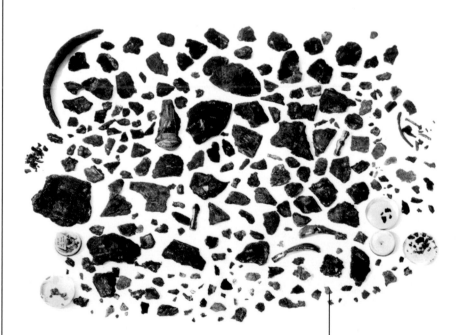

Jigsaw puzzle
More than 500 rusty metal fragments made up the historical jigsaw puzzle. Shown here are the fragments laid out before the second reconstruction in 1968.

The helmet was crushed into pieces when the burial chamber collapsed.

REPLICA OF THE HELMET

The crest had animal heads with garnet (red gemstone) eyes.

Pieces were placed on a supporting clay model.

A rigid mask was attached to the helmet to protect the warrior's face.

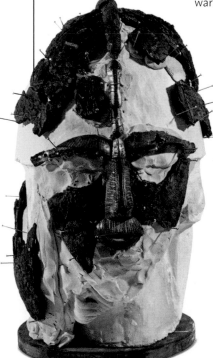

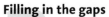

Piecing together

The helmet was rebuilt by matching the thickness, texture, and design of the various pieces. The pieces were held in place by pins on a mannequin's head.

Filling in the gaps

To complete the reconstruction, the gaps on the model were filled and painted brown to match the iron. It took an expert a year to finish the task.

MOSAIC MAKING

In 79 CE, Mount Vesuvius erupted, covering the ancient Roman city of Pompeii in a blanket of volcanic ash, trapping it in time. In 1831, archaeologists excavating the site discovered a 2nd-century BCE mosaic depicting a battle between Alexander the Great and Darius III of Persia. The original is now kept in the Naples National Archaeological Museum, but in 2003, a team at the International Center for the Study and Teaching of Mosaic in Ravenna, Italy, set about creating a replica.

▶ Roman restoration

Attempting to create an identical replica of this enormous mosaic was a huge undertaking. Nevertheless, mosaic expert Severo Bignami and his team of eight technicians got to work. Using a huge photograph as their reference (shown here hanging in the background), they started to recreate this ancient masterpiece. Their replica is now displayed in the House of the Faun in Pompeii, Italy, the site of the original excavation.

Piece by piece

Bignami and his team wanted their replica to use the same materials as the original, as well as match its size and shape. This complicated process took them 22 months, but the result is a remarkably accurate reproduction.

Tracing the photo
The team began by tracing over a photograph of the mosaic with dark marker pens. This was then pressed onto clay, creating an outline, which acted as a guide for where to place each of the two million mosaic pieces.

Cutting the tiles
To be as accurate as possible, the team cut around two million mosaic tiles, known as *tesserae*, that matched the colors and sizes of those used in the original mosaic.

Placing the tiles
Using tweezers, tiles were individually placed onto wet clay. The team recreated the huge mosaic in 44 separate sections, working on each part individually before putting them all together at the end.

THE LASCAUX CAVES

Museums often make replicas of objects so visitors can interact with the past without damaging priceless original artifacts. When the ancient cave paintings in the Lascaux cave system in the Dordogne region of France started to show signs of damage, the conservators didn't just recreate the paintings—rather, the entire cave, so that visitors could marvel at the breathtaking works of art in their natural environment, without damaging the fragile originals.

Signs of damage

This 18,000-year-old cave painting on a wall inside the Lascaux cave system is showing signs of damage. Black and white fungi as well as green algae were identified on the walls of the original caves, caused by water vapor and carbon dioxide from the breath of the 1,200 tourists that were visiting daily. The original caves are now closed to the public, and any conservators that do enter to inspect the caves' condition must do so wearing sterile coveralls.

Lascaux II, III, and IV ▶

The first replica, known as Lascaux II, opened in 1983, showing reconstructions of 90 percent of the original artwork. Lascaux III, built in 2012, refers to five replicas that were created for different museums around the world. In 2016, a new-and-improved replica opened, known as Lascaux IV. Thanks to modern computer surveying and design technology 98 percent of the artwork and 1,500 engravings are now displayed in a larger and more user-friendly space.

MAKING THE REPLICA CAVE WALLS

REPRODUCING THE ANCIENT PAINTINGS

Recreating a cave

Lascaux IV was developed over three years, using a skillful combination of technology and hard work. Three-dimensional digital scanning allowed the conservators to build an exact replica with a margin of error of only ⅛ in (3 mm). A team of 34 artists made the walls using fiberglass, resin, and polystyrene. Prehistoric pigments were re-created to hand-paint almost ½ mile (1 km) of reproductions.

BUILDING A DINOSAUR

In 2013, the 95-million-year-old bones of a *Spinosaurus*, the largest known carnivorous dinosaur, were unearthed in Morocco. Researchers discovered that the meat-eating *Spinosaurus* spent most of its time in water, making it the first known aquatic dinosaur. By scanning each existing bone and creating missing bones using photos and sketches from other specimens, they were able to digitally remodel the dinosaur to build a life-size replica of its skeleton, shown here.

Skull model

The model of the *Spinosaurus's* skull was difficult to make because the scientists only had some pieces of the original skull to work from. They used scans of these pieces as a starting point, applying their knowledge of the skulls of similar predators to recreate the skull in its entirety. They used a computer program to design the reconstruction of the skull, complete with its long jaw full of sharp teeth.

SHOW AND TELL

A museum usually only displays a small fraction of the thousands, or perhaps even millions, of items in its collection. When a museum is putting together an exhibition, curators are the masterminds who decide exactly what should go on display to best tell the story. Displaying items can be a risky business, and museums have to be careful to keep everything safe—from protecting fragile objects from damage while they are being moved to securing valuable items from theft when they are on display.

ROLES BEHIND THE SCENES
CURATOR

Curators are the guardians of museum collections. They are responsible for finding out as much as possible about the artifacts and specimens in their collections and for improving the way they are stored, cared for, and displayed. Curators help plan and organize the objects that museums have on display to the public. In some museums, they are also in charge of teaching visitors about their collections.

Planning an exhibition
One of the most important jobs of a curator is deciding which objects will be featured in an exhibition and how everything will be displayed. Here, curators at the Smithsonian's National Museum of Natural History, Washington, D.C., are working together to plan the museum's 2019 "Deep Time" exhibition.

Telling a story

Curators are responsible for creating a story about the objects they present to the public. To put on an exhibition, they work with conservators to carefully plan the display of the objects, making sure they explain the importance of each one. They guide visitors through an exhibition from start to finish using information boards with detailed descriptions about the objects on show. This curator at The Postal Museum in London, UK, is adding a postcard to an exhibition display.

▶ First-hand account

Anne Frank's diary gives us a unique insight into the persecution that Jewish people faced during World War II. As she and her family hid in an attic with four other Jewish people, she wrote about the constant fear and hardship of living under Nazi occupation, as well her private thoughts and dreams. Anne Frank wrote in this checkered diary and, when it was full, several other notebooks. Her last entry is dated August 1, 1944, three days before her capture, and less than a year before she died in Bergen-Belsen concentration camp.

Anne Frank was given her first diary for her 13th birthday on June 12, 1942.

ANNE FRANK'S DIARY

ANNE FRANK'S DIARY

Anne Frank wrote the diary in Dutch, but she also spoke German, as well as some English and French.

Personal documents like letters and diaries are valuable historical records. They reveal the private thoughts and emotions of people who lived before us and record historical events from an individual's point of view. One of the world's most famous diaries is that of Anne Frank, a Jewish girl who kept a diary for two years while in hiding from the Nazis in the Netherlands during World War II. After Anne Frank's capture, her diary and other writings were kept safe by a helper, Mies Gies, who later gave it to her father, Otto. He made a compilation of Anne's diary, her rewritten diary texts, and some short stories. He then arranged for it to be published in 1947. It has since been translated into more than 70 languages.

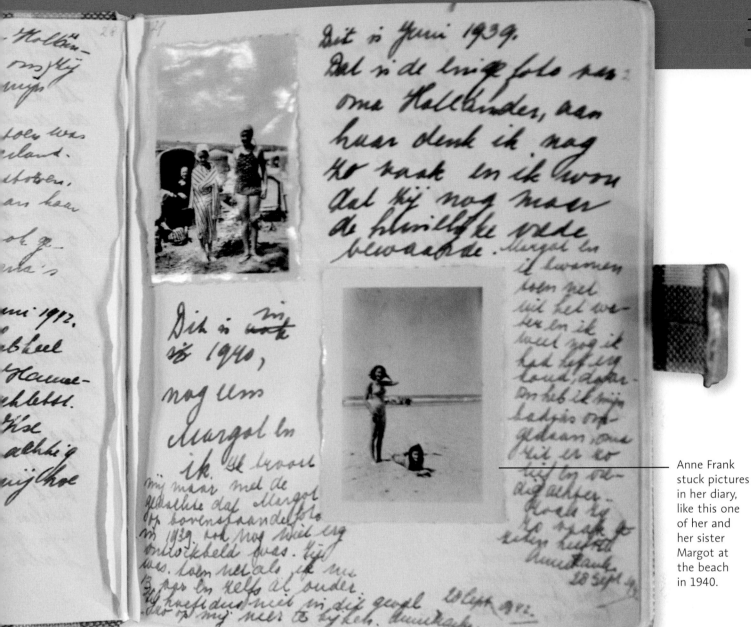

Anne Frank stuck pictures in her diary, like this one of her and her sister Margot at the beach in 1940.

Bespoke display case

The manuscripts of Anne Frank's diary are stored in several climate-controlled display cases at the Anne Frank House in Amsterdam in the Netherlands. The display cases have an inner and an outer section, with a space between them. This space is filled with cool air to maintain a temperature of 63°F (17°C) so that the manuscripts' condition does not deteriorate. Preserving the manuscripts in good condition will mean that future generations can learn about Anne Frank's story.

A pillow inside the inner case absorbs any vibrations caused by visitors walking past.

The inner case is sealed with a moisture-absorbing substance.

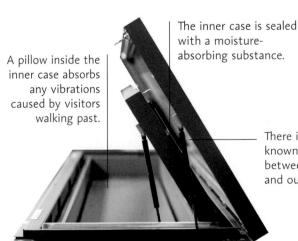

There is a space, known as a cavity, between the inner and outer cases.

CREATING A DISPLAY

At Frankfurt's Natural History Museum in Germany, putting together the *Fascination of Diversity* display in 2019 was a huge task, requiring cooperation across many of the museum's departments. Curators started the process by developing the concept of the exhibit, which was to focus on the diversity of nature, and choosing specimens to represent that concept. They then worked with designers to create detailed plans about what the exhibition space should look like, before briefing a team of construction workers to build it. Finally, the curators arranged the artifacts in the space, providing detailed information about each one.

Building a frame
Once the concept and design plans were finalized, the construction phase began. Carpenters started to create a wooden framework for the exhibition space.

Object placement
This fish skeleton has been placed upright on a mount so visitors can easily view it. If it were laid flat on the shelf, it would be much more difficult to see.

The display is designed to pack in lots of artifacts without being overwhelming.

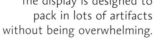

▶ Completing the display
The arrangement of the specimens was carefully planned to make the exhibit as interesting and user-friendly as possible. As more and more artifacts are added, the display began to take shape.

Assessing specimens

Curators checked over the specimens they had chosen to go on display. The selection included a wide range of objects to showcase the diversity of the museum's extensive collection.

Putting things together

Paneling, cases, and integrated lights were installed around the wooden frame, and the first specimens were put in place. The fragile specimens needed to be handled with great care.

THE FASCINATION OF DIVERSITY

From the Senckenberg Nature Research Society's enormous collection of around 40 million items, curators had to pick just 1,140 biological and geological artifacts to go on display in the *Fascination of Diversity* exhibit. The objects displayed in the 49-ft- (15-m-) long and 13-ft- (4-m-) wide exhibition space ranged from tiny beetles to large river dolphins, and together they told a story about our planet's incredible diversity.

Interactive information

Most museums display information on labels next to their artifacts and specimens, but the *Fascination of Diversity* exhibit took a different approach. Instead, it used interactive information screens. Visitors could touch a digital image of the specimen they were interested in to learn more about it.

HYENA HOME

Dioramas are three-dimensional models that replicate scenes from nature or history. They can be small enough to fit on a table or large enough that they are life-size. Museums sometimes use dioramas to introduce visitors to the habitats of animals from around the world. Creating an accurate replica is a team effort that requires expert researchers and skilled artists, as shown in this hyena diorama in the Field Museum in Chicago. The team that created it reproduced the habitat of four striped hyenas caught during an 1896 expedition to Somaliland, Africa, led by Carl Akeley, an American zoologist, taxidermist, and museum conservator.

▶ Hyena pack

This diorama shows the four taxidermied hyenas in a scene set on August 6, 1896. The diorama took months to prepare, as every detail was checked by experts—from geologists to biologists—before being handmade and painted. Astronomers even confirmed the precise positions of the stars in the night sky on that specific date.

Making the diorama

To reproduce the hyenas' habitat, the glass photographic negatives from the expedition were studied for information about the plant species that should be included in the scene. Replica plants were made from neoprene (synthetic rubber), and rocks from plaster and wire.

Small-scale model
Museum artist Adam Delehanty created an initial 1:10 scale model, which included a painted backdrop, using expert advice to make the model as realistic as possible.

Full-size diorama
The full-size display was created in the Field Museum's William V. Kelley Hall. The hyenas were then transferred to the scene, completing the landscape.

Dino find

Trix's bones, along with the surrounding rock, weighed over 5 tons. It was a big challenge for paleontologists to excavate and transport her from the desert in Montana, where she was found, to her new home in Europe.

1 Paleontologists carefully excavated 80 percent of the bones that make up Trix's skeleton.

2 Trix's bones were then packed into crates, allowing her to be moved to and from each location on the European tour by plane or truck.

3 Inside the crates, every bone had a code to make it easier for museum workers to piece together the full skeleton at each location on the tour.

TRIX THE T. REX

This 67-million-year-old *Tyrannosaurus rex*, or T. rex, nicknamed Trix, is a very well-preserved dinosaur specimen, with nearly 80 percent of her bones collected. In 2013, a team of paleontologists from the Netherlands excavated these fossils from a site in Montana. They decided to take Trix's skeleton on tour, stopping at five different European cities before putting it on permanent display at the Naturalis Biodiversity Center in Leiden, Netherlands.

▶ Back to life

Paleontologists were able to find out a remarkable amount about Trix's life by examining her bones. They were able to tell that she was female, and the number of growth lines in her bones indicated that she was more than 30 years old when she died. They also found damage to some of her bones, suggesting that Trix had been in lots of fights and suffered several diseases during her lifetime.

DID YOU · KNOW?

T. rex dinosaurs were more than 15 ft (5 m) tall. Paleontologists think parts of their bodies were covered in feathers.

Sharp teeth
Densely packed teeth allowed Trix to bite and pull at her prey.

TRIX ON DISPLAY

In 2016, Trix was exhibited at the Naturalis Biodiversity Center in Leiden, Netherlands. The following year, the dinosaur was taken on tour to several European museums, as part of an exhibition known as *T. rex in Town*. Here, Trix is on display at Kelvin Hall in Glasgow, Scotland. This tour lasted until 2019, when she returned to the Naturalis Biodiversity Center where she is now on permanent display.

T. rex on tour

To achieve this ambitious tour, the skeleton was taken apart each time it moved location. Paleontologists packed the bones in foam in order to transport them safely. It then took them between one and three days to unpack and reassemble Trix in each new location.

Bones into place
Here, a paleontologist carefully reassembles Trix's rib cage before it goes on display in Glasgow.

Hanging the tail bones
The tail bones are attached to a supporting metal frame, which helps position Trix in a dynamic, lifelike pose.

Complete skeleton

The skeleton of Trix is remarkably complete. More than half of all the bones have been preserved, making it one of the three most complete skeletons ever discovered. Even more remarkable is the fact that the bones have not been deformed.

Original/reconstruction

The skeleton of Trix is remarkably complete. All that is missing are the left leg, parts of the tail, the feet and the arms. All the remaining parts of the skeleton have been retrieved. The bones of Trix's right leg were

ROLES BEHIND THE SCENES
SECURITY

Museums contain valuable, even priceless, objects, and keeping these secure from damage and theft is an important job. Although all museums hire security staff, not many of them can compete with the responsibilities of the Vatican Museum's Head Key Keeper Gianni Crea. Along with his assistants, Crea is in charge of 2,797 keys, which open some of the world's grandest exhibition spaces. Some of the keys are hundreds of years old.

DID YOU KNOW?

There are around 300 doors to unlock in the Vatican Museum each day.

Head Key Keeper Gianni Crea walks through the Vatican Museum's Gallery of Maps, part of the 4.6-mile (7.4-km) daily route he and his assistants follow each day to open the museum.

High security

Security cameras play an important role in protecting a museum's precious artifacts from vandalism and theft. High-value artifacts are prime targets, so they are protected by alarm systems and supervised by CCTV cameras. Here, security guards monitor CCTV footage at the Grand Maket Museum, Saint Petersburg.

JEWELRY THEFT

Museums contain many valuable and often priceless objects, making them a prime target for thieves. In Dresden, Germany, in 2019, thieves managed to disable the security system of the Green Vault. They made away with irreplaceable jewels from its Saxon royal collection in a dramatic heist.

▼ Cultural crime scene

In the early hours of November 25, 2019, thieves broke into the Green Vault museum in Dresden, Germany. After setting fire to the nearby power source, which deactivated the alarm system, they cut through an iron grate and broke a window to enter the museum.

GREEN VAULT, GERMANY

Founded by Augustus the Strong in 1723, the Green Vault in Germany is among the world's oldest museums and houses one of Europe's largest collections of historic artifacts and artworks. When Dresden was bombed in 1945 during World War II, the museum suffered severe damage. It wasn't fully restored until 2006.

The area outside the museum was sealed off and the museum was closed for two days while police searched the crime scene for evidence.

Stolen jewels

The thieves snatched around 100 precious artifacts estimated to be worth as much as €1 billion ($1.1 billion). Because the pieces are so recognizable, it's feared that the thieves will break up the diamond items into smaller pieces, and melt down any gold and silver, to make it easier to sell everything. This image shows just some of the jewels that were stolen.

This shoulder ornament is made up of 236 diamonds.

This star brooch represents the Order of the White Eagle, a high honor for both civilians and the military in Poland.

Almost 800 diamonds are studded into this sword and sheath set.

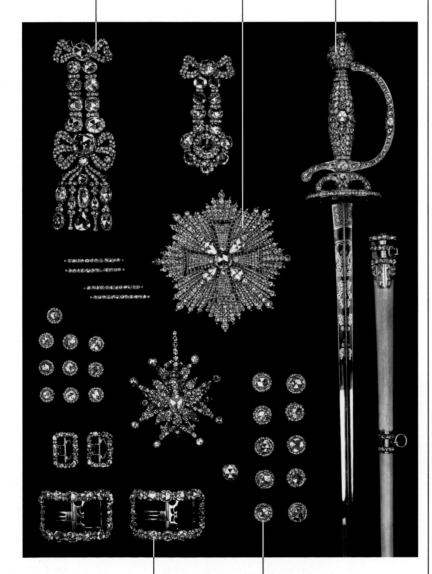

This buckle is covered in diamonds.

These buttons are inlaid with diamonds.

Investigation

Police were on the scene almost immediately thanks to the museum's security staff raising the alarm, but the thieves had already made their getaway.

Securing the premises
The iron grate that the thieves cut through was welded shut again to secure the premises.

Finding out what happened
With the museum under lockdown, police searched the scene for evidence. They suspected that the thieves had fled Dresden immediately after the heist.

Public appeal
As museum staff stressed the cultural importance of the stolen loot, police offered a €500,000 ($552,000) reward for information. Unfortunately, they haven't found the thieves or the artifacts yet.

BRILLIANT MUSEUM BUILDINGS

Museum buildings can be just as impressive as the artifacts found inside. Some are designed to tell a story about their contents, or to reflect their surroundings. Others might be old buildings that once served an entirely different purpose before becoming home to a museum's collection.

THE FORBIDDEN CITY

From the early 1400s, this vast royal complex was home to China's long line of emperors. Today, it houses a museum on Chinese history, art, and culture.

2,000,000
The approximate number of artifacts in the museum.

This huge bronze elephant statue weighs 275 tons.

THE ASHMOLEAN MUSEUM

Designed by architect Charles Cockerell, the Ashmolean Museum in Oxford, England, was the first purpose-built museum in the world. At the time, it was unusual because, unlike most museums, it opened its doors to the public.

1683
The year the museum's construction was completed.

THE ERAWAN MUSEUM

Thailand's Erawan Museum's enormous elephant sculpture isn't just for show—it's hollow and forms part of the museum's exhibition space. The building is split into three levels, representing the Underworld, the Human World, and Heaven—the Buddhist model of the Universe.

THE CAPITOLINE MUSEUM

At the top of the Capitoline Hill in Rome, Italy, sits the Capitoline Museum, which is set around a Renaissance square designed by Italian artist Michelangelo.

1734

The year the Capitoline Museum was opened by Pope Clement XII.

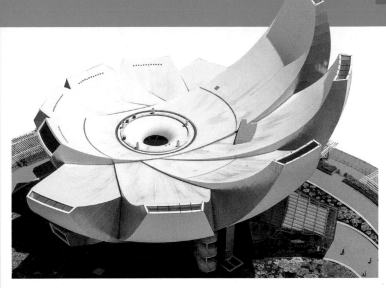

THE ART SCIENCE MUSEUM

This unusual building in Singapore was designed to look like a lotus flower, a common symbol of enlightenment and learning in Asian art. At night, colorful light shows play out over the white "petals."

2011

The year the Art Science Museum opened.

BEST OF THE REST

▶ TITANIC BELFAST, ENGLAND

This museum in Northern Ireland is dedicated to the British passenger liner RMS *Titanic*, which sank crossing the Atlantic in 1912 after hitting an iceberg. The building is designed to resemble a ship.

▶ LEGO® HOUSE, DENMARK

Full of all things LEGO®, this museum looks like it has been built using the famous bricks themselves.

▶ MUSEUM OF FIRE, POLAND

Copper paneling gives the illusion of flickering flame—fitting for a museum all about fire.

MESSNER MOUNTAIN MUSEUM

This museum of mountaineering history is located appropriately at the very top of a mountain in Italy. It has a balcony from which visitors can marvel at views of the valley below.

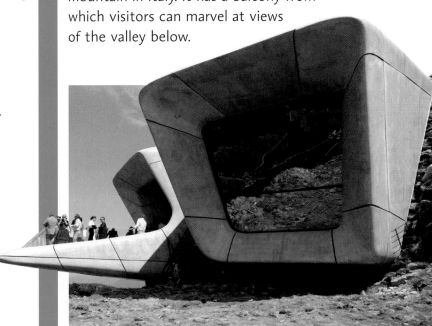

EXHIBIT CLEANING

Keeping the buildup of dust and dirt at bay is a never-ending battle for museums, and specialists are required regularly to carefully clean the displays. In particular, vintage aircraft and machinery exhibits are monitored, as dust accumulation may lead to rust or surface damage. Here, a conservator at the National Air and Space Museum in Washington, D.C., is carefully removing dust from an X-15 aircraft with a large dusting mop.

Cleaning an elephant

Dust attracts water, so it is essential to remove as much as possible from uncovered exhibits to prevent any water from staining and corroding them. A conservator uses a backpack vacuum cleaner to clean these model elephants displayed in a diorama in the Hall of African Mammals in the Natural History Museum of Los Angeles.

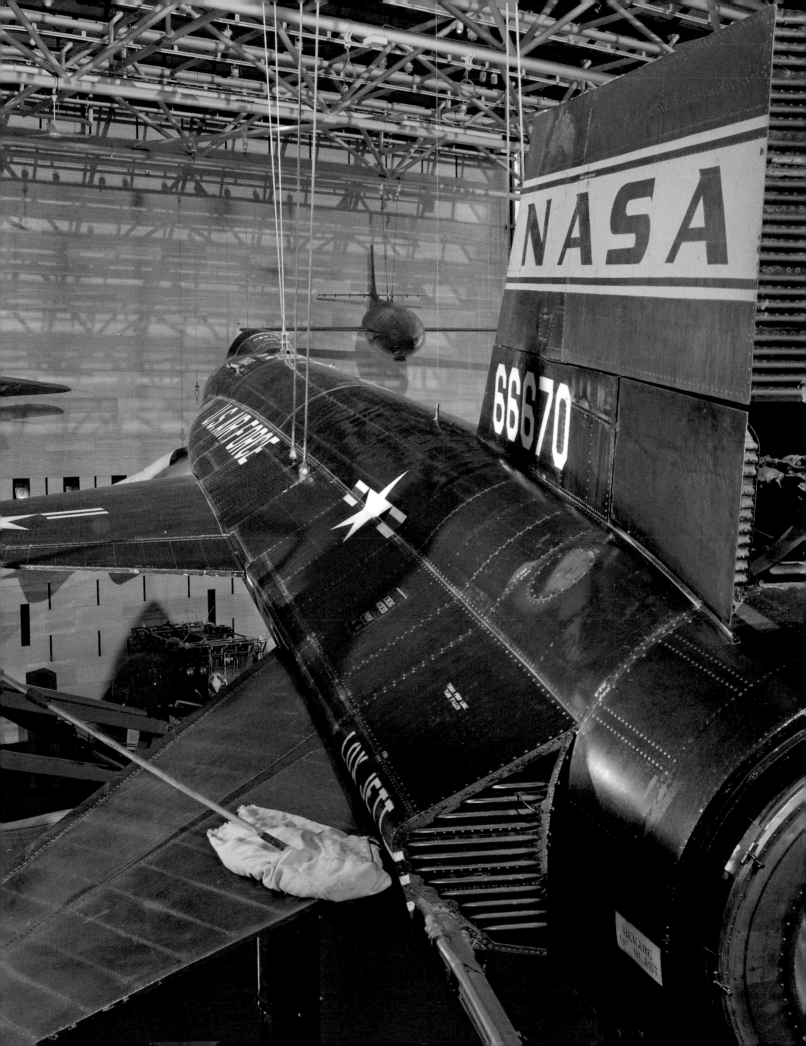

MOVING RAMSES

During the construction of the entrance hall of the Grand Egyptian Museum in Giza, Egypt, this 91-ton statue of Ramses the Great, a powerful ancient Egyptian ruler, towered over the construction workers. The enormous 39-ft (12-m) granite statue of the 19th-dynasty pharaoh is 3,200 years old, but it was stable enough to withstand the hustle and bustle of a working construction site.

Truck delivery

Engineers carefully planned how to transport the colossal statue by truck from its previous home in a temporary building to the Grand Egyptian Museum, 1,312 ft (400 m) away. The statue was moved in 2018 in a custom-built metal frame supported by two trailer beds to prevent it from being jolted by any bumps or dips in the road. Engineers also checked the road before the journey to make sure it could bear the statue's weight.

THE GRAND EGYPTIAN MUSEUM

The Grand Egyptian Museum is located near the pyramids of Giza. The museum has been designed and built to hold more than 100,000 artifacts, such as Tutankhamun's burial mask, and to welcome more than 5 million visitors every year.

HOW TO MOVE A SPACE SHUTTLE

Built in the 1970s, the first space shuttle, the *Enterprise,* didn't ever fly in space, but it was an important test vehicle for NASA's space-shuttle program. In 2012, the shuttle was transported to its new home at the Intrepid Sea, Air & Space Museum Complex located on the Hudson River in New York. This museum is situated aboard a retired World War II aircraft carrier, the USS *Intrepid.* The carefully planned operation took several months to complete.

◀ Final flight
Engineers used machines to mount the *Enterprise* shuttle on a NASA-owned, specially adapted Boeing 747 aircraft and flew it from the Smithsonian National Air and Space Museum in Washington, D.C., to New York.

Onward journey
After landing in New York, the shuttle was placed onto a barge, which transported it down the Hudson River toward the Intrepid Sea, Air & Space Museum.

Lifting into place
It took four hours to lower the spacecraft by crane onto *Intrepid*'s steel-reinforced flight deck. The shuttle weighs 150,000 lb (68,000 kg)—the weight of 12 elephants.

Building the shuttle's shelter
Once in place aboard the museum ship, a huge metal structure was built around the shuttle to protect it from the weather.

New home
The shuttle's new home, the gray building shown here, is known as the Space Shuttle Pavilion. Outside, next to it, is Concorde, the world's fastest commercial aircraft.

GLOSSARY

3-D printer
A machine that prints computer-generated, three-dimensional (3-D) representations of objects.

alum
A salt that is sometimes used as a fixative in dyeing. Its chemical name is potassium aluminium sulphate.

anthropology
The study of societies and cultures and how they live now and lived in the past.

archaeologist
A person who studies human history by excavating ancient or historic sites and the buildings and remains found there.

archaeology
The study of historic people and societies through the objects they leave behind.

Arctic
A cold region that surrounds the North Pole. It includes most of Greenland and parts of North America, Europe, and Asia.

aristocracy
A privileged ruling class of people in some societies.

artifact
A human-made object of historical interest. Artifacts allow us to find out more about the skills of the people who made them and the lives of those who used them.

binding
The covering of a book that holds all the pages together.

bronze
Bronze is a mixture of copper and tin.

Civil Rights Movement
During the mid-20th century, many people in the US came together to demand equality for African Americans.

climate change
Long-term changes in Earth's weather patterns.

contamination
Made impure by the introduction of other elements.

corrosion
The gradual deterioration of a metal due to the chemical reaction between air and water.

conservation
Conservation work in museums is carried out to help protect and care for objects, including paintings, documents, and textiles.

consort
The spouse of a ruling queen or king.

crop marks
Reveal buried archaeological sites that cannot be seen from the ground.

curator
A person who manages a collection of historical artifacts or works of art, oversees exhibitions to attract and educate visitors.

donation
Something that is given to a museum or another organization. Donations are often in the form of artifacts or money.

drone
A type of flying machine that does not require a pilot. Someone on the ground controls it.

element
In science, a pure substance, such as gold, hydrogen, or oxygen, that is made up of only one kind of atom.

ethnicity
Communities of people that share a common ancestry, culture, language, religion, and nation.

evolution
The gradual change in a species over many generations.

excavating
Digging out and removing fossils or other objects from the ground.

exposure
Having no protection from the rain, wind, Sun, or other elements.

extinct
When all members of a species of living thing have died out, they are said to be extinct.

flagship
A ship that carries the commanding officer or admiral of a fleet of warships. Through history, it was often the largest, most decorated, and most heavily armed vessel in the fleet.

fossil
The remains or impression of a prehistoric plant or animal, often preserved in rock.

funerary
Objects or processes associated with funerals and burying the dead.

geology
The study of Earth's structure, especially the rocks that form the solid parts of Earth.

hazmat suit
A protective garment worn when dealing with hazardous materials.

humidity
The amount of water vapor in the air.

indigenous
Originating from a particular place.

lacquer
A synthetic protective coating for wood that hardens as it dries.

magnification
The number of times the naked-eye view of an object is enlarged when seen through a microscope, telescope, or binoculars.

meteorite
A piece of rock or metal from space that enters Earth's atmosphere and reaches the ground without burning up.

monument
A building, structure, or statue built to honor an important person or event. Any unique architecture can also be called a monument.

off-gassing
When synthetic materials produce acidic gases that can cause damage.

paleontologist
A person who studies prehistoric species.

permafrost
Ground that remains permanently frozen beneath the topsoil.

pest
A destructive insect.

pigment
A natural coloring in animals or a substance used to produce color for art.

plinth
A platform such as a column on which a statue or artifact stands.

prehistoric
The time before written records were made.

preservation
Looking after an object by stopping deterioration and preventing future damage.

provenance
The place of origin and history of ownership of an artifact or object.

Prussia
A small state in today's northeast Germany, which rose to become a great European power in the 1700s.

quarantine
A period of isolation to prevent insects, germs, or diseases from spreading.

radioactive
Relating to atoms that are unstable and break apart, releasing high-energy particles.

registrar
A person who is responsible for keeping track of museum artifacts in storage and in transport.

repatriation
The process of returning something (such as an artifact) back to its country of origin.

replica
An exact copy of something, such as a statue.

restoration
The process of returning something to its original condition.

sandblasting
The process of vigorously removing dirt and rust by firing a stream of sand at high pressure onto a surface.

specimen
A natural sample of a species of plant, animal, or mineral used by researchers for study.

synthetic
Something that is made of artificial material.

tar
A thick, sticky substance formed either naturally from crude oil or by processing crude oil or coal. Natural tar is usually called bitumen.

taxidermy
The process of preparing and stuffing the remains of an animal in order to preserve it and give it a lifelike appearance.

tomb
A building or grave used for a burial.

UNESCO World Heritage Site
An area that has been selected by the United Nations Educational, Scientific and Cultural Organization (UNESCO) for having historical or scientific importance. As a result, the site is given funds and protected from development.

visitor services
The staff members at a museum who deal directly with the public, such as information desk staff and tour guides.

INDEX

Page numbers in **bold** refer to main entries.

ACKNOWLEDGMENTS

DK would like to thank the following people for their contribution:
Victoria Pyke for proofreading; Helen Peters for indexing; Ben Morgan for additional writing; Shaila Brown and Mani Ramaswamy for additional editing; Samantha Richiardi and Sunita Gahir for additional design; Jess Cawthra for research; Steve Crozier for picture retouching; Jacket Designers Priyanka Bansal, Tanya Mehrotra, Suhita Dharamjit; Senior DTP Designer Harish Aggarwal; Jackets Editorial Coordinator Priyanka Sharma; and Managing Jackets Editor Saloni Singh.

Smithsonian Enterprises:
Kealy Gordon, Product Development Manager; Jill Corcoran, Director, Licensing Publishing; Brigid Ferraro, Vice President, Consumer and Education Products; Carol LeBlanc, President.

Smithsonian Curators:
National Museum of Natural History:
Matthew T. Miller, Museum Specialist, Department of Paleobiology; Steve Jabo, VP Prep Lab, Department of Paleobiology; Abby Telfer, Museum Program Specialist, Department of Paleobiology; Jeff Post, Chair of the Mineral Science Department; Lucia Martino, Contract Photographer, Office of Photography and Media.

National Museum of American History:
Jennifer L. Jones, Project Director, Curatorial Affairs.

National Air and Space Museum:
Erik Satrum, Chief Registrar; Cathy Lewis, Curator, Space History Department.

Smithsonian Institution Archives:
William Bennet, Conservator.